DISCOVERING CAREERS FOR YOUR FUTURE

teaching

SECOND EDITION

Ferguson
An imprint of Infobase Publishing

Discovering Careers for Your Future: Teaching, Second Edition

Ferguson
An imprint of Infobase Publishing
132 West 31st Street
New York NY 10001

Library of Congress Cataloging-in-Publication Data

Discovering careers for your future. Teaching. — 2nd ed.
    p. cm.
  Includes bibliographical references and index.
  ISBN-13: 978-0-8160-7292-7 (alk. paper)
  ISBN-10: 0-8160-7292-2 (alk. paper)
  1. Teaching—Vocational guidance—United States—Juvenile literature. 2. Teachers—Training of—United States—Juvenile literature.
  LB1775.2.D58 2008
  371.10023'73
                                    2007046147

Ferguson books are available at special discounts when purchased in bulk quantities for businesses, associations, institutions, or sales promotions. Please call our Special Sales Department in New York at (212) 967-8800 or (800) 322-8755.

You can find Ferguson on the World Wide Web at http://www.fergpubco.com

Text design by Mary Susan Ryan-Flynn
Cover design by Jooyoung An

Printed in the United States of America

EB MSRF 10 9 8 7 6 5 4 3 2 1

This book is printed on acid-free paper.

Contents

Introduction

You may not have decided yet what you want to be in the future. And you don't have to decide right away. You do know that right now you are interested in teaching. Do any of the statements below describe you? If so, you may want to begin thinking about what a career in education might mean for you.

___I enjoy going to school every day.
___I have leadership qualities.
___I am good at explaining things to other people.
___I enjoy babysitting and being with young children.
___I am good at public speaking.
___I like to lead discussions.
___I am interested in learning new things every day.
___I like to get other people interested in my hobbies (music, sports, computers, or photography, for example).
___I enjoy homework assignments that involve preparing oral presentations.
___If I learn something quickly in class, I am eager to help my classmates understand.

Discovering Careers for Your Future: Teaching is a book about careers in education, from adult and vocational education teachers to teacher aides. Teachers of younger students usually teach a wide variety of subjects and skills, including reading, writing, math, and getting along with others. Teachers of older students tend to specialize in one subject, such as math or history. College-level teachers may specialize even more and teach only American history or African-American history. Some teachers focus on educating a special group of people, such as people with disabilities, or those who don't speak English. Teachers do not work just in schools, but in businesses, industries, museums, and parks. Some teachers become interested in the education process and work in administration and planning.

This book describes many possibilities for future careers in teaching. Read through it and see how the different careers are connected. For example, if you are interested in working with young children, you will want to read the chapters on child care workers, elementary school teachers, English as a Second Language teachers, preschool teachers, special education teachers, and teacher aides. If you are interested in teaching adults, you will want to read the chapters on adult and vocational education teachers, career counselors, college professors, and computer trainers. If you want to teach music, then you will want to read the chapter on music teachers. If you would like to work as a teacher outside of a school setting, you will want to read the chapters on museum attendants and teachers and naturalists. Go ahead and explore!

What Do Teachers Do?

The first section of each chapter begins with a heading such as "What School Administrators Do" or "What Education Directors Do." It tells what it's like to work at this job. It describes typical responsibilities and assignments. You will find out about working conditions. Which teachers work in traditional classrooms? Which ones work in nontraditional settings? This section answers all these questions.

How Do I Become a Teacher?

The section called "Education and Training" tells you what schooling you need for employment in each job—a high school diploma, training at a junior college, a college degree, or more. It also talks about on-the-job training that you could expect to receive after you're hired, and whether or not you must complete an apprenticeship program.

How Much Do Teachers Earn?

The Earnings section gives the average salary figures for the job described in the chapter. These figures give you a general idea of how much money people with this job can make. Keep in mind that many people really earn more or less than the amounts given here because actual salaries depend on many different things, such as the size of the school, the location of the school, and the amount of education, training, and experience you have. Generally, but not always, bigger schools located in major cities pay more than smaller ones in smaller cities and towns, and people with more education, training, and experience earn more. Also remember that these figures are current averages. They will probably be different by the time you are ready to enter the workforce.

What Will the Future Be Like for Teachers?

The Outlook section discusses the employment outlook for the career: whether the total number of people employed in this career will increase or decrease in the coming years and whether jobs in this field will be easy or hard to find. These predictions are based on economic conditions, the size and makeup of the population, foreign competition, and new technology. Phrases such as "faster than the average," "about as fast as the average," and "slower than the average," are used by the U.S. Department of Labor to describe job growth predicted by government data.

Keep in mind that these predictions are general statements. No one knows for sure what the future will be like. Also remember that the employment outlook is a general statement about an industry and does not necessarily apply to everyone. A determined and talented person may be able to find a job in an industry or career with the worst kind of outlook. And a person without ambition and the proper training will find it difficult to find a job in even a booming industry or career field.

Where Can I Find More Information?

Each chapter includes a sidebar called "For More Info." It lists organizations that you can contact to find out more about the field and careers in the field. You will find names, addresses, phone numbers, e-mail addresses, and Web sites.

Extras

Every chapter has a few extras. There are photos that show teachers in action. There are sidebars and notes on ways to explore the field, fun facts, profiles of people in the field, or lists of resources that might be helpful. At the end of the book you will find three additional sections: Glossary, Index of Job Titles, and Browse and Learn More. The Glossary gives brief definitions of words that relate to education, career training, or employment that may be unfamiliar to you. The Index of Job Titles includes all the job titles mentioned in the book. The Browse and Learn More section lists general education books and Web sites to explore.

It's not too soon to think about your future. We hope you discover several possible career choices. Happy hunting!

Adult and Vocational Education Teachers

What Adult and Vocational Education Teachers Do

Adult and vocational education teachers teach classes for adults and high school students. Older students take classes to prepare for better jobs or for advanced education. They might take courses to improve skills they already have or to learn new technologies. Adult education teachers lead classes, assign reading, and help students develop technical and academic skills.

Adult education teachers in basic education programs teach students school subjects like English, math, and composition. In vocational training programs, they teach trades such as automobile repair or carpentry. They also work within companies, training employees for specific job positions. In community colleges, they teach subjects as varied as airplane flying, computer programming, foreign language, and oil painting.

Adult education teachers may teach one person at a time or a large classroom of students. Classes may take place in a laboratory, a shop, or at actual work sites. Adult and vocational education teachers prepare for classes the same way as any other kind of teacher. They

The Community College Connection

The American Association of Community Colleges conducted a survey to find how many members of the U.S. Congress have a connection to community colleges. Whether as a teacher, student, or board member, 60 of the 535 members of Congress had some direct connection with community colleges. The survey found that 29 members of the 109th Congress had earned an associate's degree from a community college, and 12 members had taught at a community college.

EXPLORING

○ Some of your teachers may be teaching adult or vocational education courses in the evenings; talk to them about the difference between teaching middle school or high school and teaching in an adult education program.

○ Volunteer to tutor peers or younger students. Your school or community center may have volunteer tutoring opportunities.

○ Volunteer to assist in special educational activities at nursing homes, churches or other religious organizations, or community centers. For example, you might be able to teach senior citizens how to use the Internet or teach a foreign student to speak English.

decide what books and other learning materials to use. They prepare a daily schedule, give lectures, and lead class discussions. They prepare and give exams, and grade essays and presentations. Some industries require teachers to cover specific subjects if students must pass strict industry tests that qualify them for career advancement.

Education and Training

Adult education teachers usually focus on a specific subject. They become teachers because of their expertise gained through education, on-the-job training, work experience, and personal interest.

In high school, take courses that best suit your teaching interests. You'll also need to follow a college preparatory plan, taking courses in English, math, foreign language, history, and government. Speech and communications courses will help you prepare for speaking in front of groups of people. Writing skills are very important, no matter what subject you teach, because you'll be preparing reports, writing lesson plans, and grading essays. In most states, teachers of adult basic education must have a bachelor's degree in education. Some states also require a teaching certificate. Vocational instructors need to have practical experience in the skills they are teaching. Some professions require vocational teachers in their field to have a teaching license or certificate. For some subjects teachers need no special certification or training in education, but they need to be extremely knowledgeable in their field.

The Top 10

These are the top 10 certificates and associate's degrees awarded by community colleges in the 2004–2005 academic year, according to the National Center for Education Statistics.

Certificate	Number Awarded
1. health professions and related sciences	86,875
2. business, management, and marketing	25,827
3. security and protective services	19,675
4. mechanics and repairs	14,305
5. transportation and material moving workers	11,918
6. computer and information sciences	10,865
7. family and consumer sciences	10,636
8. engineering-related technologies	7,677
9. personal and culinary services	6,172
10. construction trades	5,691

Associate's Degree	Number Awarded
1. liberal-general studies and humanities	240,131
2. health professions and related sciences	122,520
3. business, management, and marketing	96,067
4. computer and information sciences	36,173
5. engineering-related technologies	35,989
6. security and protective services	23,749
7. visual and performing arts	22,650
8. personal and culinary services	16,311
9. multi-interdisciplinary studies	13,888
10. mechanics and repairs	13,619

Earnings

Full-time adult and vocational education teachers earned an average of $43,910 a year in 2006, according to the U.S. Department of Labor. In general, full-time instructors earned salaries

FOR MORE INFO

For information on publications, contact
**American Association for Adult and
Continuing Education**
10111 Martin Luther King Jr. Highway
Suite 200C
Bowie, MD 20720
Tel: 301-459-6261
http://www.aaace.org

For information on the field, contact
**Association for Career and Technical
Education**
1410 King Street
Alexandria, VA 22314-2749
Tel: 800-826-9972
E-mail: acte@acteonline.org
http://www.acteonline.org

*For information about government pro-
grams, contact*
U.S. Department of Education
Office of Vocational and Adult Education
400 Maryland Avenue SW
Washington, DC 20202-7100
Tel: 202-245-7700
E-mail: ovae@ed.gov
http://www.ed.gov

that ranged from less than $24,610 to $75,680 or more per year, with some highly skilled and experienced teachers earning even higher salaries. Earnings vary widely according to the subject, the number of courses taught, the teacher's experience, and the location.

About half of all adult and vocational education teachers teach part time. They are often paid by the hour. Hourly rates range from $6 to $50.

Outlook

Employment opportunities in adult education are expected to grow as fast as the average, according to the U.S. Department of Labor. Adults know they need to keep learning to succeed and advance in today's workplace. In fact, many courses are paid for by companies that want their employees trained in the latest skills and technology of their field. The biggest growth areas will be in computer technology, automotive mechanics, and medical technology. Major employers of adult and vocational education teachers will be vocational high schools, private trade schools, community colleges, and private adult education enterprises.

Athletic Trainers

What Athletic Trainers Do

Athletic trainers help athletes stay healthy and avoid injuries. They work with injured athletes to get them back into competitive shape. The professional athletic trainer may work with a team of physicians, physical therapists, and dietitians to plan a program of health maintenance for team athletes. Their main purpose is to keep the athletes competitive and fit. The trainer's program includes exercise, weight lifting, relaxation and meditation, and controlled diet.

If an athlete is injured, the trainer is in charge of treating the injury and helping the athlete recover completely. Athletic trainers work with physicians and coaches to decide if the athlete should continue to compete or not. Where the athlete is to compete, how important the event, and how extensive the injury

Where Do Athletic Trainers Work?

- ○ secondary schools
- ○ colleges and universities
- ○ professional sports teams
- ○ hospitals, clinics, physicians' offices, and sports medicine clinics
- ○ industrial and commercial settings
- ○ performing arts centers
- ○ the military
- ○ law enforcement facilities

Source: National Athletic Trainers' Association

EXPLORING

○ Learn about nutrition and how diet affects both physical performance and mental stamina.

○ Participate in school and community sports programs.

○ Take classes in first aid and CPR. Check with your local American Heart Association or Red Cross chapter for course schedules.

○ Participate in physical fitness programs offered at your YMCA or YWCA, park district, or local gym. Try different types of training, including aerobics, weight training, and stretching.

○ Talk to an athletic trainer about his or her career. Ask the following questions: What do you like least and most about your job? How did you train for this field? What advice would you give a young person who is interested in the field?

are all factors in the decision. A trainer may decide to let a runner continue training with a sprained ankle if the Olympics trials are days away. If there is only a small competition coming up, the trainer may recommend that the athlete take a few weeks off to recover. The trainer designs a series of exercises that rebuild strength without damaging or straining the injured area.

Athletic trainers work hard to prevent injuries. They recommend running, stretching, weight lifting, and other exercise programs to help athletes stay in good physical condition and make their bodies stronger. Athletic trainers may also design workout programs to strengthen weaker body parts, such as ankles and elbows, to reduce the likelihood of injury.

During competition, trainers treat minor injuries, such as cuts and bruises. They use ice, bandages, and other first aid to reduce swelling and help athletes cope with pain. For more serious injuries, such as a bad sprain or broken bone, trainers make sure that the athletes receive proper medical attention.

Trainers recommend hot baths, do massage, administer whirlpool treatment, wrap injured areas, and use other techniques to speed the athlete's recovery.

Education and Training

To become an athletic trainer you need a bachelor's degree in physical education, physical therapy, or another area

How Sports Injuries Are Classified

○ A *minor injury* is one that causes a player to be removed from the remainder of the current session (practice or game). The player returns to activity within seven days.

○ A player who suffers a *moderate injury* is removed from the current session and does not return to activity for eight to 21 days.

○ A player with a *major injury* is removed from the current session and does not return to activity for more than 21 days.

related to health care. Trainers should take courses in first aid, anatomy, nutrition, and physical therapy in addition to general courses in health and the sciences, especially biology and chemistry.

Facts About Injuries to High School Athletes

More than half of injuries to high school athletes in nine sports were found to occur during practice sessions, according to a study released by the National Athletic Trainers' Association. The sports studied were baseball (boys), softball (girls), football (boys), field hockey (girls), soccer (both), basketball (both), volleyball (girls), and wrestling (boys). The data came from 246 certified athletic trainers representing different-sized schools across the country. The results of this study showed these discoveries:

○ Football had the highest rate of injuries, while volleyball showed the lowest rate.

○ The largest number of fractures came from boys' baseball, basketball, soccer, and softball, in that order.

○ More than 73 percent of injuries required players to stop competing fewer than eight days.

○ The highest frequency of knee injuries occurred in girls' soccer.

○ The largest proportion of surgeries reported among the 10 sports was for girls' basketball and the lowest was field hockey. Most of the injuries requiring surgery were knee injuries.

FOR MORE INFO

To obtain publications about sports medicine, contact
American College of Sports Medicine
PO Box 1440
Indianapolis, IN 46206-1440
http://www.acsm.org

For information on certification, contact
Board of Certification
4223 South 143rd Circle
Omaha, NE 68137-4505
Tel: 877-262-3926
E-mail: staff@nataboc.org
http://www.bocatc.org

For career information and a list of accredited athletic training programs, contact
National Athletic Trainers' Association
2952 Stemmons Freeway Suite 200
Dallas, TX 75247-6115
Tel: 214-637-6282
http://www.nata.org

Earnings

The U.S. Department of Labor reports that athletic trainers earned median salaries of $36,560 in 2006. The highest 10 percent earned more than $57,580, while the lowest 10 percent earned less than $21,940.

According to the National Association for Sport and Physical Education, salaries for athletic trainers in schools range from $25,000 to $35,000. With experience and a master's degree, college trainers can earn up to $45,000 to $60,000 per year. Athletic trainers who work for professional sports teams earn salaries ranging from $60,000 to $125,000. Some trainers work all year while others work only during the playing season. Trainers who work for schools usually earn a teacher's salary plus an additional amount for their training duties.

Outlook

As sports continue to grow in popularity, there should be a need for more skilled athletic trainers. However, many people want to enter this field, so those with the best education and training will have the most success finding a job. Trainers who want to work for professional sports teams will face the most job competition but will also earn the highest salaries. A master's degree is usually required to gain these top positions.

Career Counselors

What Career Counselors Do

Career counselors help people discover their occupational interests and skills and guide them in career decisions. First, counselors get to know their clients and what their goals, abilities, and interests are. Counselors sometimes give tests, including achievement and aptitude tests. The results of the tests and personal interviews with the clients help career counselors identify possible career choices for them.

Counselors suggest education and training programs if the client needs them. They teach job-hunting strategies, such as responding to newspaper ads, doing Internet searches, and sending out résumés and cover letters. Counselors might teach how to approach interviews, and how to discuss salary and benefits with potential employers.

Vocational-rehabilitation counselors work with disabled individuals to help the counselees understand what skills they have to offer to an employer.

College career planning and placement counselors work exclusively with the students of their universities or colleges. They may specialize in some specific area appropriate to the students and graduates of the school, such as law and education, as well as in part-time and summer work, internships, and field placements.

Why Someone Might Need a Career Counselor

- ○ layoffs
- ○ relocation
- ○ technological advances that change work tasks
- ○ lack of advancement opportunities
- ○ divorce
- ○ retirement
- ○ insufficient salary
- ○ change in interests
- ○ job dissatisfaction
- ○ prison release

EXPLORING

○ Explore Internet job-search sites like Monster (http://www.monster.com), CareerBuilder (http://www.careerbuilder.com), and Yahoo Hot-Jobs (http://www.hotjobs.com).

○ Look at the Help Wanted section of your newspaper. Most newspapers run these ads every day and have an expanded job section on Sundays. If you live in a small city or town, you might want to take a look at a newspaper from a large city, such as New York, Chicago, or Los Angeles. Choose some job categories that interest you and find out what the typical education, experience, and personal requirements are for jobs in that category.

○ Learn library skills, such as researching, cataloging, and filing.

○ Interview a career counselor or a director of a public or private employment agency to get a better understanding of the pros and cons of the field.

Employment counselors might also work with employers to help them hire people for specific job openings. They gather descriptions of the particular positions that employers need to fill and find qualified candidates for employers to interview.

Career counselors have enormous responsibilities as they assist people in making major life decisions. They need thorough knowledge of education, training, employment trends, the job market, and career resources.

Career counselors are assisted by *career guidance technicians,* who collect pertinent information to support both the counselor and applicant during the job search.

Education and Training

In high school, in addition to studying a core curriculum, with courses in English, history, mathematics, and biology, you should take courses in psychology and sociology. You will also find it helpful to take business and computer science classes.

To be a career counselor you must usually have a master's degree and complete a period of supervised counseling before you can practice on your own. A doctorate is generally recommended for the best jobs. New career counselors are often considered trainees for the first 6 to 12 months of their employment. They may work for schools or colleges, for

Career Counseling Timeline

○ The first funded employment office in the United States was established in San Francisco in 1886.

○ In 1908, the Civic Service House in Boston began the first program of vocational guidance, and the Vocational Bureau was established to help young people choose, train for, and enter appropriate careers.

○ In 1910, a national conference on vocational guidance was held in Boston. The federal government gave support to vocational counseling by initiating a program to assist veterans of World War I in readjusting to civilian life.

○ During the Great Depression, agencies such as the Civilian Conservation Corps and the National Youth Administration offered vocational counseling.

○ On June 6, 1933, the Wagner-Peyser Act established the United States Employment Service.

○ State and federal government agencies now involved with vocational guidance services include the Bureau of Indian Affairs, the Bureau of Apprenticeship and Training, and the Department of Education.

public health agencies, in business or industry, or have their own private practices.

Earnings

The median yearly earnings for educational, vocational, and school counselors were $47,530 in 2006, according to the U.S. Department of Labor. The lowest paid 10 percent of these workers earned $27,240 per year, and the highest paid 10 percent made $75,920 or more annually. Those in business or industry can earn higher salaries.

Outlook

Opportunities in the field of employment counseling are expected to grow faster than the average, according to the U.S. Department of Labor. One reason for this growth is increased

FOR MORE INFO

For of career resources for career seekers and career counseling professionals, contact the following organization:

American Counseling Association
5999 Stevenson Avenue
Alexandria, VA 22304-3304
Tel: 800-347-6647
http://www.counseling.org

For résumé and interview tips, general career information, and advice from experts, visit the following Web site:

National Association of Colleges and Employers
62 Highland Avenue
Bethlehem, PA 18017-9481
Tel: 800-544-5272
http://www.naceweb.org

For information on certification, contact

National Board for Certified Counselors
3 Terrace Way
Greensboro, NC 27403-3660
Tel: 336-547-0607
E-mail: nbcc@nbcc.org
http://www.nbcc.org

school enrollments, even at the college level, which means more students needing the services of career counselors. Another reason is that there are more counselor jobs than graduates of counseling programs. Opportunities should also be available in government agencies as many states institute welfare-to-work programs or simply cut welfare benefits. Finally, more career counselors will be needed because workers today don't have as much job security as they did in the past. Others are reentering the workforce after having children or leaving their jobs for other reasons. And some people are simply deciding to try a new career and need information on how to do so.

Child Care Workers

What Child Care Workers Do

Child care workers work with infants, toddlers, and preschool-aged children at day care centers, preschools, or other child care facilities. They watch young children and help them develop skills through games and activities.

Child care workers at larger centers may have more structured activities. They read to the children, guide arts and crafts projects, and teach them songs. They help preschoolers

It Takes All Kinds

The National Association of Child Care Resource and Referral Agencies lists these types of child care providers:

○ **family child care** is a service in which a child care worker cares for unrelated children in his or her own home.

○ a **for-profit chain center** is a corporation that may operate only a few centers in a single community, or more than 1,000 across the country.

○ an **independent for-profit center** is a center individually owned and operated.

○ an **independent nonprofit center** is a small community center focused primarily on serving poor families.

○ a **church-housed center** is based in a church, offering services to the community at large.

○ a **Head Start Center** is funded by the federal government and serves three- and four-year-olds on a part-time basis.

EXPLORING

○ There are many volunteer opportunities that will give you experience in working with children. Check with your library or local literacy program about tutoring children and reading to preschoolers. Summer day camps, religious schools, children's theaters, museums, and other organizations with children's programs may also need volunteer assistants.

○ Talk to neighbors, relatives, and others with small children about babysitting during evenings and weekends.

○ Talk to a child care worker about his or her career. Ask the following questions: What are your main and secondary job duties? What do you like least and most about your job? How did you train for this field? What advice would you give a young person who is interested in the field?

develop basic skills, such as recognizing letters, numbers, and colors. Child care workers lead children in simple tasks, such as cleaning up after themselves, picking up toys, and washing their hands.

A child care worker should know basic first aid and be able to react quickly in emergency situations. Child care workers provide a nutritious midday meal and occasional snacks. They also make sure children take naps or have quiet times during the day.

Child care workers must follow the wishes of parents. They provide parents with reports on their children's progress and behavior and notify them immediately if there are any problems. It is just as important to have a good relationship with the parents as it is to get along with the children.

Education and Training

In high school, you should take child development, home economics, and other classes that involve you with child care. You should also take courses in English, art, music, and theater to develop your creative skills.

To be a child care worker, you need a high school diploma and some child care experience. Requirements vary among employers, though. Some employers prefer to hire workers who have taken college courses in child development, or hold bachelor's degrees. You may earn better wages if you have some college education.

Child care workers should love and respect children and have a genuine interest in their well-being. (Jim West, The Image Works)

Safety Concerns for Kids

cribs: Older cribs and mattresses that are too small can cause strangulation and suffocation. Cribs must meet current national safety standards and be in good condition.

bedding: Sudden Infant Death Syndrome (SIDS) and suffocation are sometimes related to the use of pillows, soft bedding, or comforters. Babies should be put to sleep on their backs in a crib with a firm, flat mattress.

playground surfaces: Children can suffer injuries from falls, especially head injuries, when playground surfaces are too hard. Outdoor playgrounds should have at least 12 inches of wood chips, mulch, sand, or pea gravel, or mats made of safety-tested rubber or rubber-like materials.

safety gates: Safety gates, especially on stairs, can protect against many hazards, especially falls.

window blind and curtain cords: Children can be strangled in the loops of window blind and curtain cords. Miniblinds and venetian blinds should not have looped cords. Vertical blinds, continuous looped blinds, and drapery cords should have tension or tie-down devices to hold the cords tight.

clothing drawstrings: Drawstrings can catch on playground and other equipment and strangle young children. Be sure there are no drawstrings around the hood and neck of children's outerwear.

FOR MORE INFO

For information on accredited programs, contact

National Association for the Education of Young Children
1313 L Street NW, Suite 500
Washington, DC 20005-4110
Tel: 800-424-2460
http://www.naeyc.org

For information about student memberships and training opportunities, contact

National Association of Child Care Professionals
PO Box 90723
Austin, TX 78709-0723
Tel: 800-537-1118
E-mail: admin@naccp.org
http://www.naccp.org

For information about certification and to learn about the issues affecting child care, contact

National Child Care Association
2025 M Street NW, Suite 800
Washington, DC 20036-3309
Tel: 800-543-7161
E-mail: info@nccanet.org
http://www.nccanet.org

Earnings

According to the U.S. Department of Labor, child care workers earned about $8.48 an hour in 2006, which amounts to yearly earnings of about $17,630 for full-time work. Annual salaries ranged from less than $12,910 to $27,050 or more a year.

Outlook

Employment of child care workers should increase about as fast as the average, according to the U.S. Department of Labor. Many positions become available because these workers don't stay in their jobs very long. One of the main reasons for this is the low pay.

More child care centers, both non-profit and for-profit, are expected to open in the next few years as more mothers take jobs outside the home and need child care services. There will be more jobs available with franchises and national chains, as well as with centers that cater exclusively to corporate employees. Bilingual child care workers will find more job opportunities and better salaries.

College Administrators

What College Administrators Do

College administrators develop and manage services for students in colleges and universities. Administrators arrange housing; special services for veterans, minorities, and students with disabilities; and social, cultural, and recreational activities. The following paragraphs detail some of most common types of administrators.

College presidents are the top administrators. Their duties include overseeing academic programs, planning budgets, hiring and firing faculty and other staff, and fund-raising.

The *dean of students* heads the entire student-affairs program. *Associate* or *assistant deans* may be in charge of specific aspects of student life such as housing. *Academic deans* handle such issues as course offerings and faculty.

Directors of college admissions review records, interview prospective students, and process applications for admission.

Registrars prepare class schedules, make room assignments, keep records of students and their grades, and gather data for government and educational agencies.

Financial aid administrators, also known as *directors of student financial aid,* oversee the scholarship, grant, and loan programs that provide financial assistance to students and help them meet

Who's in Charge?

College administrators include:

○ vice presidents of business, student services, or academic affairs
○ controllers
○ housing directors
○ directors of the physical plant
○ human resources directors
○ directors of student activities
○ admissions directors
○ directors of financial aid
○ directors of security and safety
○ purchasing directors
○ directors of college unions
○ directors of food services

EXPLORING

○ To learn something about what the job of administrator entails, talk to your high school principal and superintendent. Also, interview administrators at colleges and universities.

○ Work in student government positions or serve as chair for clubs you belong to. This will provide you with both management and administrative experience.

○ Familiarize yourself with all the various aspects of college life by looking at college student handbooks and course catalogs (available at your library or on the Internet). Most handbooks list all the offices and administrators and how they assist students and faculty.

the costs of tuition, fees, books, and other living expenses. The administrator keeps students informed of the financial assistance available to them and helps answer student and parent questions and concerns. At smaller colleges, the *financial aid officer* might do all of this work. At larger colleges and universities, the staff might be bigger, and the financial aid officer heads a department and directs the activities of *financial aid counselors,* who handle most of the personal contact with students.

The *director of student activities* helps student groups plan and arrange social, cultural, and recreational events. Other student-affairs administrators include the *director of housing,* who manages room assignments and the upkeep of dormitory buildings. *Directors of religious activities* coordinate the activities of various religious groups.

Foreign-student advisers work with foreign students and give special help with admissions, housing, financial aid, and English instruction. The *director of the student health program* hires staff and manages the health care center and its equipment. *Athletic directors* are in charge of all intercollegiate athletic activities. They hire coaches, schedule sports events, and direct publicity efforts.

Education and Training

To prepare for a job in college administration, take accounting and math courses in high school, as you may be dealing

To Be a Successful College Administrator, You Should . . .

- be very organized and able to manage a busy office of assistants
- be a good leader
- have good people skills
- have patience and tact to handle a wide range of personalities
- be very organized
- have strong communication skills

with financial records and student statistics. To be a dean of a college, you must have good communication skills, so you should take courses in English literature and composition. Also, speech courses are important, as you'll be required to give presentations and represent your college at meetings and conferences.

To be a college administrator, you need a well-rounded education that prepares you for college. For most college administration jobs, you need at least a bachelor's degree. For the top positions, you need a master's or doctoral degree in administration, business, or education. For these positions, you must also have many years of experience at a college or university as a lower-level administrator, or as a professor and department chair.

Earnings

Salaries vary greatly for college administrators and depend on the college's location, whether it is a two- or four-year institution, and whether it is public or private. According to the U.S. Department of Labor, the median salary for education administrators was $73,990 in 2006. The lowest paid 10 percent of

College Stats, 2006

○ There were 4,216 colleges and universities in the United States.

○ Approximately 17,648,000 students were enrolled.

○ Fifty-eight percent of college students were women.

○ The average tuition at private four-year institutions was $22,218.

○ The average tuition at public four-year institutions was $5,836.

○ The average tuition at public community colleges was $2,272.

Source: *Chronicle of Higher Education*

administrators earned $41,120 or less per year, while the highest paid made $137,900 or more annually.

The College and University Professional Association for Human Resources, reports the following median salaries for college administrators by profession: academic dean, $68,774 (continuing education) to $362,508 (medicine); college president, $207,999; director, student health services (physician), $137,709; chief admissions officer, $75,920; director of student financial aid, $68,000; registrar, $66,008.

Outlook

The number of college-age students is expected to increase, so more jobs may open in the field. However, leaner budgets are currently making the job market in college administration competitive. Most job openings will be to replace workers who are retiring or leaving their jobs.

The U.S. Department of Labor predicts there will be strong competition for college administrator positions. Most administrative jobs are filled by faculty who have gained the necessary education and experience. Budgetary problems have forced some colleges and universities to reduce administrative jobs. Opportunities will be best for those who are interested in working in nonacademic administrative positions, such as director of admissions or director of student affairs.

FOR MORE INFO

For information on careers in college admin- istration, contact the following organizations:

American Association of Collegiate Registrars and Admissions Officers
One Dupont Circle NW, Suite 520
Washington, DC 20036-1148
Tel: 202-293-9161
http://www.aacrao.org

American Association of University Administrators
PO Box 630101
Little Neck, NY 11363-0101
Tel: 347-235-4822
http://www.aaua.org

Association of College Administration Professionals
PO Box 1389
Staunton, VA 24402-1389
Tel: 540-885-1873

E-mail: acap@cfw.com
http://www.acap.org

College and University Professional Association for Human Resources
2607 Kingston Pike, Suite 250
Knoxville, TN 37919-3331
Tel: 865-637-7673
http://www.cupahr.org

National Association of College and University Business Officers
1110 Vermont Avenue NW, Suite 800
Washington, DC 20005-3593
Tel: 800-462-4916
http://www.nacubo.org

National Association of Student Personnel Administrators
1875 Connecticut Avenue NW, Suite 418
Washington, DC 20009-5737
Tel: 202-265-7500
http://www.naspa.org

College Professors

What College Professors Do

College and university faculty instruct students at two- and four-year colleges and universities. *College professors* have three main responsibilities: teaching, advising, and conducting research. Professors give lectures, lead discussions, give exams, and assign reading and term papers. They may spend fewer than 10 hours a week in the classroom, but they spend many hours preparing lectures and lesson plans, grading papers and exams, and preparing grade reports. They also meet with students individually outside of the classroom to guide them in the course and to keep them updated about their progress.

Some faculty members also work as student advisers, helping students decide which courses to take, informing them of requirements for their majors, and directing them toward scholarships and other financial aid. They may also help students adjust to college life.

Many college professors conduct research in their field of study and publish the results in textbooks and journals. They attend conferences and present research findings to professors from other universities.

Distance learning programs are an increasingly popular option for students. They give professors the opportunity to use today's technologies (computers, the Internet, e-mail, and video conferencing) to remain in one place while teaching students who are at a variety of locations. Professors who do this work are sometimes known as *extension work, correspondence,* or *distance learning instructors.*

The Most Popular Bachelor's Degrees

At Public Colleges
1. business
2. social sciences
3. education
4. psychology
5. health professions and related clinical sciences
6. communications, journalism, and related programs
7. engineering
8. visual and performing arts
9. biological and biomedical sciences
10. English language and literature

At Private Colleges
1. business
2. social sciences
3. visual and performing arts
4. education
5. psychology
6. health professions and related clinical sciences
7. computer and information sciences
8. communications, journalism, and related programs
9. biological and biomedical sciences
10. English language and literature

Source: U.S. Department of Education, 2003–2004

The *junior college instructor* has many of the same kinds of responsibilities as does the teacher in a four-year college or university.

Education and Training

During your middle- and high-school years, you should concentrate on a college preparatory program and focus on your particular interest. When you finish your undergraduate degree

EXPLORING

○ Talk to your teachers about their careers and their college experiences.

○ Volunteer with a community center, day care center, or summer camp to get teaching experience.

○ Look at course catalogs and read about the faculty members and the courses they teach. These are available at your library and on the Internet at a college's Web site.

and enter a master's or doctoral program, you will probably be required to take on some assistant-teaching responsibilities.

To teach in a four-year college or university, you must have at least a master's degree. With a master's degree you can become an instructor. You will need a doctorate for a job as an assistant professor, which is the entry-level job title for college faculty. Faculty members usually spend no more than six years as assistant professors. During this time, the college will decide whether to grant you tenure, which is a type of job security, and promote

Information Security on Campus

The 2007 Campus Computing Project survey shows that Information Security is becoming a key issue on college campuses. Overall, the single most important Information Technology (IT) issues on campus in 2007 were network and data security (25.5 percent); upgrade/replace emergency resource protocols (13.0 percent); and hiring/retaining IT staff (12.3 percent). Here are few additional results from the survey:

○ 59.1 percent of institutions reported that they had a strategic plan for IT disaster recovery, up from 55.7 percent in 2006 and 55.4 percent in 2004.

○ 60.1 percent of colleges have wireless networks, up from 51.2 percent in 2006 and 31.1 percent in 2004.

○ 14.8 percent of institutions reported major problems with computer viruses, down from 35.4 percent in 2005.

○ 45.6 percent of institutions reported hacks or attacks on campus networks, down from 51.1 percent in 2005.

you to associate professor. An associate professor may eventually be promoted to full professor.

Earnings

The American Association of University Professors reported the average yearly income for all full-time faculty was $73,207 in 2006–2007. It also reported that professors earned the following salaries by rank: full professors, $98,974; associate professors, $69,911; assistant professors, $58,662; lecturers, $48,289; and instructors, $42,609.

Outlook

The U.S. Department of Labor says there should be much-faster-than-average growth for college and university professors. College enrollment is projected to grow due to an increased number of 18- to 24-year-olds, an increased number of adults returning to college, and an increased number of foreign-born students. Competition will be especially strong for full-time, tenure-track positions at four-year universities. Opportunities for college teachers will be especially good in engineering, business, computer science, and health science.

Women Professors Earn Less than Men

A report by the American Association of University Professors (AAUP) shows that female professors do not earn as much as male professors and have fewer positions in the higher ranks. The AAUP found that female professors earned 12.3 percent less ($89,591) than male professors ($102,128) in 2006–2007.

FOR MORE INFO

To read about the issues affecting college professors, contact the following organizations:

American Association of University Professors
1012 14th Street NW, Suite 500
Washington, DC 20005-3406
Tel: 202-737-5900
http://www.aaup.org

American Federation of Teachers
555 New Jersey Avenue NW
Washington, DC 20001-2029
Tel: 202-879-4400
http://www.aft.org

Computer Trainers

What Computer Trainers Do

Today's employees and students need to know how to send e-mail, how to use the Internet, and how to use word processing programs. However, many people become frustrated when faced with a blank computer screen and a thick instruction manual. Sometimes, too, the computers and programs are too complex to be explained fully and clearly by a manual. *Computer trainers* teach people how to use computers, software, and other new technology. When a business installs new hardware and software, computer trainers work one on one with the

Teaching Techniques

Here are some techniques that trainers use to keep the attention of their students:

case study a presentation of hypothetical (imaginary) scenarios to practice problem-solving skills

demonstration a presentation to learners of how to perform a task

expert panel a group of experts sharing their ideas with each other and the audience

games contests and matches used to improve technical performance and to encourage teamwork

programmed instruction trainees working through a series of steps that help them learn specific skills

role play two or more individuals acting out a situation that might occur in the real workplace to practice interpersonal skills

Source: The American Society for Training and Development

employees, or they lead group training sessions. They may also offer instruction over the Internet. With technology changing every day, computer trainers are called upon often for support and instruction.

Computer trainers teach people how to use computer programs. For example, a company's accounting department may hire a computer trainer to teach its accounting clerks how to use a spreadsheet program, which is used to make graphs and charts, and to calculate sums. Other common business programs include database programs, which keep track of such things as customer names, addresses, and phone numbers, and word processing programs, which are used to create documents, letters, and reports. Some computer trainers may also teach computer programming languages such as COBOL, FORTRAN, PASCAL, RPG, CSP, C++, or Java.

EXPLORING

○ Visit your local library or bookstore and surf the Internet to keep up with the latest software and technology. The Internet has thousands of sites on computers and computer training.

○ Teach yourself as many software packages as you can.

○ Teach new programs to your parents, grandparents, or younger sisters and brothers.

Many corporations, advertisers, and individuals have set up Web sites. A computer trainer can help them use the computer language needed to design a page, and teach them how to update the page. Trainers teach people how to operate desktop publishing programs and laser printers that allow individuals and businesses to create interesting graphics and full-color pages for brochures and newsletters. Some computer trainers may also help offices set up their own office network. With a network, all the computers in an office can be linked. Employees then share programs and files, conference with other employees, and send e-mail.

Computer trainers may be self-employed and work on a freelance basis, or they may work for a computer training school or computer service company.

Education and Training

Take as many computer and mathematics classes as possible in high school. These will provide the foundation for the rest of your computer education. Speech, drama, or other performance courses will also help get you used to speaking in front of a crowd.

Most community colleges, universities, and vocational schools offer computer courses. Computer service companies and training schools also offer courses in specific software programs. Though college courses and training are important, it helps to have experience, too. You can get experience by working with computers on a regular basis, either at home or in the workplace. You can also gain computer experience by working in the sales department of a computer store or software company.

Education requirements vary at computer training schools and computer service companies. To work as a teacher in

The History of Computing on the Web

Computer History
http://www.computerhope.com/history

Computer History: Tracing the History of the Computer
http://www.computernostalgia.net

Computer History Collection
http://americanhistory.si.edu/collections/comphist

Computer History Museum
http://www.computerhistory.org

Computer Industry History
http://www.elsop.com/wrc/h_comput.htm

The Virtual Museum of Computing
http://vmoc.museophile.org

a high school or community college, a bachelor's degree is the minimum requirement.

Earnings

The average training specialist earns about $45,000. Senior training specialists average $60,000 a year, and training managers earn about $75,000. According to a 2005 salary survey conducted by *Microsoft Certified Professional Magazine,* the average salary of responding Microsoft Certified Trainers was $68,535. These figures do not include yearly bonuses, which may add several thousand dollars to a trainer's income. In general, salaries for computer trainers increase with the level of education.

Outlook

The outlook for computer trainers is excellent because more people are using computers and related technology than ever before. According to the American Society for Training and Development, the short life cycles of technology products, combined with the greater complexity of many job roles, will increase the demand for computer trainers.

FOR MORE INFO

For a list of academic programs and resources in the computer training field, contact
American Society for Training and Development
1640 King Street, Box 1443
Alexandria, VA 22313-2043
Tel: 703-683-8100
http://www.astd.org

For more information on computer training, contact
ITrain, International Association of Information Technology Trainers
PMB 616
6030-M Marshalee Drive
Elkridge, MD 21075-5987
Tel: 888-290-6200
http://itrain.org

Education Directors

What Education Directors Do

Education directors help museum and zoo visitors learn more about the exhibits they have come to see. Education directors plan and develop educational programs. These programs

A Day in the Life of an Education Director

7:30 A.M.—Arrive at the museum. Check in at the security station and pick up identification badge.

7:45 A.M.—Settle in office. Return phone calls and e-mail.

9:00 A.M.—Attend meeting with anthropology and history curators, exhibit designers, and museum taxidermist. Discuss plans for upcoming exhibit. Focus on exhibit design that will best represent objects and include thought-provoking interpretation for museum visitors.

10:30 A.M.—Give tour of rainforest exhibit to second graders.

12:00 P.M.—Give lunch lecture on Native American cradleboards to Civic Foundation members.

1:00 P.M.—Lunch.

1:30 P.M.—Give tour of Egyptian exhibit to high school students.

2:45 P.M.—Meet with education staff to develop ideas for instructional materials to use with the upcoming exhibit. Focus on materials for self-guided tours, families, and teachers.

4:15 P.M.—Return phone calls and e-mail messages. Open mail.

5:15 P.M.—Prepare budget material for tomorrow's meeting with the director of finance and the museum director.

6:00 P.M.—Stop at the security station and turn in badge.

include tours, lectures, and classes that focus on the history or environment of a particular artifact or animal.

For example, a museum or zoo might focus on helping children understand more about the exhibits. In museums, children often are allowed to handle artifacts or play with objects. In zoos, children may be able to pet animals. Education directors develop special projects to help visitors learn more from this type of hands-on experience.

Education directors give teachers advice on how to lead workshops and classes. They help resource directors find materials, such as eggshells or skeletons, and instruments, such as microscopes, to use in their resource centers. Working with exhibit designers to create displays, they might show the development of a moth into a butterfly, or display tools and artifacts used by ancient Egyptians. They also work with graphic designers to produce signs and illustrations that reveal more about an exhibit. Signs in a gorilla exhibit, for instance, may include a map of Africa to show where gorillas live.

Most education directors at museums work in art, history, or science, but other museums have a special interest, such as woodcarvings or circuses. Directors of these museums must have some training or experience in special fields, just as the people overseeing zoos must know about animals. Wherever they work, education directors must have a good knowledge of all the specimens in their collection.

EXPLORING

○ Most zoos and museums have student volunteers. Volunteers often help with tours, organize files or audiovisual materials, or assist a lecturer in a class.

○ The American Association of Museums (http://www.aam-us.org) publishes an annual museum directory, a monthly newsletter, and a bimonthly magazine. It also publishes *Careers in Museums: A Variety of Vocations* and *Museums: A Place to Work—Planning Museum Careers.* This report is helpful for anyone considering a career in the museum field.

○ *Introduction to Museum Work,* published by the American Association for State and Local History (http://www.aaslh.org), discusses the educational programs at various museums.

Education and Training

In high school, you should take courses in creative writing, literature, history of world civilizations, American history, science, foreign language, art, and speech. Math and computer skills are also strongly recommended.

Education directors usually begin in another position at a zoo or museum, perhaps as a teacher or resource coordinator. They are usually promoted to the position, or transfer between organizations to reach the director level. Education directors must have at least a bachelor's degree. Most positions require a master's degree, and many, including those at larger zoos and museums, require a doctorate.

Education directors often earn a bachelor's degree in liberal arts, history, or one of the sciences. They go on to earn a graduate degree in a specialized area of education.

Earnings

Salaries for education directors vary depending on the size, type, and location of the institution, as well as the director's education and experience. According to Salary.com, 50 percent of education specialists who were employed at museums earned between $36,389 and $49,739 in 2007. Salaries ranged from less than $31,463 to $56,969 or more annually.

To Be a Successful Education Director, You Should . . .

○ have excellent communication skills
○ be able to motivate and teach people from a wide range of cultural backgrounds, age groups, and educational levels
○ be organized
○ have strong leadership skills

Outlook

Employment for education directors is expected to increase more slowly than the average, according to the U.S. Department of Labor. Many museums and cultural institutions have cut their budgets and reduced the size of their education departments. Competition will be stiff for jobs in large cities and in well-known, popular institutions.

FOR MORE INFO

This organization provides information and training through publications, annual meetings, seminars, and workshops.

American Association for State and Local History
1717 Church Street
Nashville, TN 37203-2991
Tel: 615-320-3203
http://www.aaslh.org

For a directory of museums and other information, contact

American Association of Museums
1575 Eye Street NW, Suite 400
Washington, DC 20005-1113
Tel: 202-289-1818
http://www.aam-us.org

For a directory of internships offered through public gardens, contact

American Public Gardens Association
100 West 10th Street, Suite 614
Wilmington, DE 19801-6604
Tel: 302-655-7100
http://www.aabga.org

Elementary School Teachers

What Elementary School Teachers Do

Elementary school teachers plan lessons, teach a variety of subjects, and keep student records. Elementary school usually includes kindergarten through the fifth grade.

Elementary teachers instruct about 20 to 30 students in the same grade. In the early grades, they teach basic skills in reading, writing, counting, and telling time. With older students, they teach history, geography, math, English, and handwriting. In some elementary schools, there are special teachers for art, music, and physical education.

Teachers use a variety of aids to instruct their students. These aids include the computer and Internet, textbooks, workbooks, magazines, newspapers, maps, charts, and posters. Teachers must have a love of learning and be enthusiastic about working with children.

Before and after school, teachers spend time planning classes. They grade papers, tests, and homework assignments, and they prepare student reports.

Teachers work with the school principal to solve problems, set up field trips, and plan school assemblies. They meet with parents to keep them informed about their child's progress, and with school psychologists and social workers to help students with learning difficulties and other problems.

Education and Training

In high school, you should take advanced courses in English, math, science, history, and government.

All public schoolteachers must be college graduates who are certified by the state in which they want to teach. In college, you should major in education. You will spend several weeks as a student teacher in an actual elementary school classroom. Your college program will lead to state certification. Some states may require you to take additional certification tests after graduating from an education program.

Earnings

According to the American Federation of Teachers, beginning teachers earned average salaries of $31,753 a year in 2004–2005. The median annual salary for elementary school teachers was $45,570 in 2006, according to the U.S. Department of Labor. The lowest 10 percent earned $30,370 or less; the highest 10 percent earned

EXPLORING

○ Your school may have a program for older students to tutor younger students in reading or math.
○ Volunteer to teach Sunday school classes or become an assistant in a scout troop.
○ Look for opportunities to coach children's athletic teams.
○ Your local community theater may need directors and assistants for summer children's productions.
○ Teach a younger sister or brother to read and write.
○ Talk to your teacher about his or her career.

Public School Facts, 2003–2004

○ More than 61 percent of elementary and secondary school teachers were female.
○ The average school year was 132 days.
○ States with the most elementary school students: California, Florida, Georgia, Illinois, Michigan, New York, Ohio, Pennsylvania, and Texas.
○ States with the fewest elementary school students: Alaska, Delaware, Montana, North Dakota, South Dakota, Vermont, and Wyoming.

Source: U.S. Department of Education

A Brief History

The history of elementary education goes back to the people of Judah, who established schools for young children in synagogues about 100 B.C. as part of the children's religious training.

In the early days of Western elementary education, the teacher only had to complete elementary school to be qualified to teach. School terms were generally about six months. The school building was often small, poorly heated, and badly lit. Many elementary schools combined all grades into one room, and the course of study was the same for everyone. In these early schools, the teacher was not well paid and had little recognition in the community.

When people decided that teachers should be better educated, the normal school—a school designed to train teachers—was established. The first normal school, opened in Concord, Vermont, in 1823, was a private school. The first state-supported normal school was established in Lexington, Massachusetts, in 1839. By 1900, nearly every state had at least one state-supported normal school.

FOR MORE INFO

To read about the issues affecting teachers, contact the following organizations:

American Federation of Teachers
555 New Jersey Avenue NW
Washington, DC 20001-2029
Tel: 202-879-4400
http://www.aft.org

National Education Association
1201 16th Street NW
Washington, DC 20036-3290
Tel: 202-833-4000
http://www.nea.org

$72,720 or more. Private school teachers generally earn less than public school teachers.

Outlook

According to the *Occupational Outlook Handbook*, employment for teachers (grades K–12) is expected to grow as fast as the average. The need to replace retiring teachers will provide many opportunities nationwide. There will be a greater demand for teachers in inner-city schools and for those with specialties in math, science, and foreign language.

English as a Second Language Teachers

What ESL Teachers Do

English as a Second Language (ESL) teachers teach people of all ages the English language. Most students are immigrants and refugees. Some may be children of foreign-born parents, or children living in a home where English is not spoken.

Many public and private schools employ ESL teachers. They do not necessarily speak the language of the students they are instructing. However, many teachers try to learn some key words and phrases in their students' native tongues in order to communicate better.

The main goal of ESL teachers is to help students learn to use the English language to communicate in both speech and writing. In the classroom they use many different teaching methods including games, videos, DVDs, computers, field trips, role-playing, and other activities to make learning fun and interesting. Classes often center on teaching conversation skills, telephone skills, the art of listening, and the idioms of the English language. The instructor helps students learn correct pronunciation, sentence structure, vocabulary, composition, and punctuation.

Our Melting Pot

According to the 2000 U.S. Census, there are more than 300 languages spoken in the United States. After English, the most common languages spoken at home for people age five and over are:

1. Spanish	6. Korean
2. Chinese	7. Russian
3. Tagalog	8. German
4. Vietnamese	9. Arabic
5. French	10. Italian

EXPLORING

○ Join a foreign language club.
○ Talk to your teachers and parents about becoming a foreign exchange student or housing a foreign exchange student.
○ Participate in community multicultural events to learn more about other cultures and languages.
○ Volunteer to help with any assistance programs that your community or church (or other religious organization) might have for immigrants or refugees.

Many ESL teachers teach adults. With the steady flow of refugees and immigrants to the United States, community centers, libraries, churches and other religious organizations, and assistance centers offer ESL classes.

ESL teachers also find many opportunities overseas, teaching English as a foreign language. Some overseas employers offer free housing, medical care, and other benefits as part of the teaching contract.

Education and Training

High school courses in English, foreign language, and social studies are highly recommended for ESL teachers.

To teach in public schools, you must be a college graduate. Some schools offer a major in ESL. You may

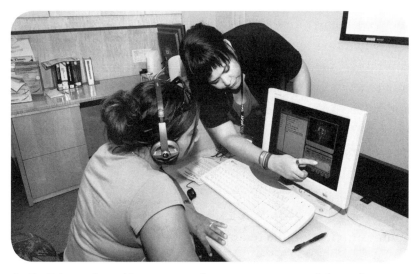

An English as a Second Language teacher uses a computer to help teach a student. (Chris Ware, The Image Works)

Think About It

Scholars believe that the English language is one of the most difficult languages to learn. What would you think if you moved to our country and you were trying to speak our language?

The words *rough, bough, cough, though,* and *through* all have the same endings, but think about how you pronounce each word.

Making words plural can really cause confusion. For instance, the plural of *man* is *men,* but the plural of *can* is *cans.* The plural of *foot* is *feet,* but the plural of *root* isn't "reet," but *roots.* The plural of *mouse* is *mice,* but the plural of *blouse* is *blouses,* not "blice."

We also have homonyms, which are words pronounced the same but meaning different things. For example, *foul* and *fowl; sight, cite,* and *site; hear* and *here;* and *to, two,* and *too.*

Our language has a large vocabulary. For example, we can eat at a restaurant, a diner, a bistro, a grill, a luncheonette, a supper club, a coffee shop, a cafeteria, a buffet, or a café.

also major in education with a concentration in ESL as a subject area.

Teachers in public schools must be licensed by the state in which they teach. ESL teachers of adult students do not need a license. There are many training programs available for ESL teachers of adults. These programs usually last from 4 to 12 weeks. When you complete the program, you receive a certificate or diploma.

Earnings

The U.S. Department of Labor reports that the median salary of adult literacy and remedial education teachers was $43,910 in 2006. Earnings ranged from

Did You Know?

Nearly 94,000 people participated in English as a Second Language classes, basic skills, or GED preparation classes in 2004–2005, according to the National Center for Education Statistics.

FOR MORE INFO

The following organizations provide information on teaching careers:

American Federation of Teachers
555 New Jersey Avenue NW
Washington, DC 20001-2029
Tel: 202-879-4400
http://www.aft.org

National Education Association
1201 16th Street NW
Washington, DC 20036-3290
Tel: 202-833-4000
http://www.nea.org

This organization has information on adult ESL literacy and offers resources and support for teachers, tutors, and others interested in the education of refugees, immigrants, and other U.S. residents whose native language is not English.

Center for Adult English Language Acquisition
4646 40th Street NW
Washington, DC 20016-1859
Tel: 202-355-1500
http://www.cal.org/caela

The following organization provides information on ESL:

TESOL (Teachers of English to Speakers of Other Languages)
700 South Washington Street, Suite 200
Alexandria, VA 22314-4287
Tel: 888-547-3369
E-mail: info@tesol.org
http://www.tesol.org/s_tesol/index.asp

less than $24,610 to more than $75,680 a year. Teachers employed at elementary and secondary schools had mean annual earnings of $53,050 in 2006. Private school teachers on average earn less than public school teachers. Earnings for ESL teachers overseas vary. Some positions are on a volunteer basis, where teachers receive no pay, but receive housing, food, and transportation. Job assignments can vary in length from a few weeks to a year or more. Wages often depend on the country's economic health. Overseas teachers consider other benefits equal to pay, such as the opportunity to live and work in a foreign culture.

Outlook

According to the American Federation of Teachers, school districts report that there is a shortage of teachers of bilingual education. The increasing immigrant and refugee populations in the United States will create demand for instruction in the English language, whether in the school system, the community, or the workplace. Many community and social service agencies, as well as community colleges, are offering assistance to immigrants and refugees and will need ESL teachers.

The U.S. Department of Labor reports that the demand for adult education teachers is expected to grow as fast as the average.

Guidance Counselors

What Guidance Counselors Do

Guidance counselors help students with college, career, and personal choices. They help students to choose their classes and teachers and to develop better study habits. They provide information and advice to students who are trying to select colleges and training programs. They supply necessary school records, write letters of recommendation, and guide students through the application process for admission and financial aid.

Guidance counselors also help students who are having trouble with educational, social, or personal problems. Sometimes suggestions and encouragement are all that students need. But if a student has a serious problem, a counselor may refer the student to a social welfare agency, child guidance

School Counselors Face New Challenges

High school counselors today help students deal with more than just academic challenges. The fact sheet, *Changing Lives, Building Futures: The Expanded Role of School Counselors*, details the following issues faced by students:

- ○ 33 percent of girls and 25 percent of boys reported feeling highly stressed.
- ○ 33 percent of students reported getting into one or more physical fights.
- ○ 15 to 25 percent of students reported being bullied with some to moderate frequency.
- ○ 5.4 percent of students reported that they skipped school in the past month because they were afraid to go to school because of violence.

EXPLORING

- ○ Visit Web sites that a guidance counselor might suggest to high school students for college information, including Embark.com, Collegebound.net, CollegeisPossible.org, and SuperCollege.com.
- ○ Your best resource for information about work as a guidance counselor is right in your own high school. Ask your school's counselor how he or she got started in the career, and about the nature of the job.
- ○ Volunteer to assist in the counselor's office, and help with career days and other events and programs.

clinic, health department, or other community-service organization.

Another important duty of guidance counselors is collecting and organizing materials for students to read about occupations, personal and social matters (such as peer pressure and self-esteem), and educational opportunities beyond high school. They hold group guidance meetings with students in which topics of special interest to the group are discussed. They also organize special days devoted to career exploration and college recruitment, inviting representatives of various occupations and colleges to the school to talk to students.

Guidance counselors help new students learn about the school and adjust to their new environment. They administer and grade standardized tests, and meet with parents, school psychologists, social workers, and other teachers to discuss individual students and school guidance programs.

Education and Training

To prepare for a career as a guidance counselor, take social studies, language arts, mathematics, and speech classes in high school.

You need to earn a bachelor's degree and complete certain specified courses at the graduate level. About three out of five guidance counselors have master's degrees. Graduate programs in counselor education include courses in career development, group counseling, and substance abuse counseling.

Most states require that counselors have a teaching certificate. You can earn a teaching certificate by taking classes during your undergraduate years.

Earnings

Wages for guidance counselors vary by region of the country, school and district size, and age of the students. Larger districts usually offer higher salaries, and counselors working with high school students tend to earn more than counselors for younger grades. The lowest salaries for guidance counselors in the United States are in the Southeast, and the highest are on the West Coast. Beginning salaries in the field averaged less than $27,240 in 2006, while the most experienced counselors earned more than $75,920. According to the U.S. Department of Labor, the average salary for educational, vocational, and school counselors was $47,530 a year in 2006.

Outlook

The federal government has called for more counselors in the schools to help address issues of violence and other dangers,

Mean Annual Earnings for Educational, Vocational, and School Counselors by Industry, 2006

Federal Executive Branch	$63,170
Elementary and Secondary Schools	$55,560
Educational Support Services	$53,910
Junior Colleges	$53,650
Colleges, Universities, and Professional Schools	$44,730
Vocational Rehabilitation Services	$34,320

Source: U.S. Department of Labor

FOR MORE INFO

For information about counseling careers and graduate school programs, contact

American Counseling Association
5999 Stevenson Avenue
Alexandria, VA 22304-3304
Tel: 800-347-6647
http://www.counseling.org

For information about careers and accredited counseling programs, contact

American School Counselor Association
1101 King Street, Suite 625
Alexandria, VA 22314-2957
Tel: 800-306-4722
http://www.schoolcounselor.org

For information about college admission counseling and a list of related publications, contact

National Association for College Admission Counseling
1631 Prince Street
Alexandria, VA 22314-2818
Tel: 703-836-2222
http://www.nacacnet.org

such as drug use. Though violence in the schools has been decreasing, the number of students afraid to go to school has increased. This increase is a result of the shootings and gang-related warfare that became headlines in the late 1990s. The government, along with counseling professionals, is also working to remove the stigma of mental illness, and to encourage more children and families to seek help from school counselors.

Technology will continue to assist counselors in their jobs. With Internet access in the libraries, counselors can easily direct students to specific career information, scholarship applications, and college Web sites. School counselors may also follow the lead of Internet counselors and offer guidance online, so students who want to remain anonymous can request information and advice from counselors through e-mail and other online services.

Math Teachers

What Math Teachers Do

Math teachers help students learn simple and advanced math theories and apply these concepts to everyday life. They work in elementary, middle, and high school classrooms.

Math teachers teach complex mathematical subjects such as algebra, calculus, geometry, trigonometry, and statistics to middle and high school students. They may teach algebra to a class of ninth graders one period and trigonometry to high school seniors the next. Teachers must be able to get along with young people, have patience, and like to help others. They need good communication skills, since they often work with students from varying ethnic backgrounds and cultures.

Math teachers not only teach specific subjects, but also must make learning fun and teach students how to work together. Math teachers encourage creative and logical thinking as it relates to math and education in general. They may use games, computers, and experiments as hands-on teaching tools in the classroom.

Math teachers also develop lesson plans, create exams, correct papers, calculate grades, and keep records. Some schools may also require teachers to lead extracurricular activities such as math club, competitions, and events. Teachers meet with and advise students, hold parent/teacher conferences, and attend faculty meetings. In addition, they may have to attend local, state, and national conferences. Teachers must take continuing education courses to maintain their state's teaching license.

Education and Training

If you want to pursue a career as a math teacher, you should take high school math courses including algebra, geometry,

EXPLORING

○ By attending your own math classes, you've already gained a good sense of the daily work of a math teacher. But teachers have many duties beyond the classroom, so ask to spend some time with one of your teachers after school. Ask about their job, how they prepared for their career, and look at their lecture notes.

○ Teach a younger sister or brother to count or do basic arithmetic, such as addition and subtraction. As they get a little older, you can teach them the value of coins and how to make change.

○ Your school or community may have a volunteer program where you can tutor younger children in math.

trigonometry, and calculus. More advanced classes in probability, statistics, and logic are also beneficial if they are available. Computer science, psychology, and English classes are also recommended.

There are more than 500 accredited teacher education programs in the United States. Most of these programs are designed to meet the certification requirements for the state in which they're located. Some states may require that you pass a test before being admitted to an education program. You may choose to major in mathematics while taking required education courses, or you may major in secondary education with a concentration in math. Although requirements for teaching licenses vary by state, all public schools require teachers to have a bachelor's degree and to complete the state's approved training program.

Earnings

According to the U.S. Department of Labor, the median annual salary for secondary school teachers was $47,740 in 2006. Salaries ranged from less than $31,760 to $76,100 or more annually. The median annual salary of middle school teachers was $46,300 in 2006. The lowest paid 10 percent of these teachers earned less than $31,450, and the top 10 percent made $73,350 or more per year. College math teachers earned $56,420 a year in 2006.

Math Is Everywhere

We use math every day in all kinds of ways. Here are some examples:

○ **Art**. Artists use triangles, squares, rectangles, circles, and other geometric shapes. Some artists use math when they create special formulas to mix their own paints, chemicals, or other materials.

○ **Music**. Rhythm is based on counting. Think of whole notes, half notes, quarter notes, and eighth notes and you are thinking in fractions.

○ **Sports**. Math is used in sports for scoring, figuring averages and percentages, and compiling statistics.

○ **Health**. Temperature, heart rate, pulse, and blood pressure all are measured in numbers. Diet and nutrition use basic math to calculate calories, fat grams, and recommended daily allowances. You use math to understand dosages for drugs.

Outlook

Teachers are generally in short supply across the nation due to rising school enrollments and the number of teachers who are retiring. Math teachers are particularly needed. According

Profile: Grace Hopper (1906–1992)

When mathematician Grace Hopper was young, her hobbies were needlepoint, reading, and playing the piano. Her father encouraged her to pursue things that interested her, even if they were considered more "masculine" pursuits. In 1943, she was sworn into the U.S. Navy Reserve, where she served for 43 years.

Hopper coined the term "bug," meaning a computer fault, while working on the Harvard Mark I computer. The real bug in the Mark I was a moth that caused a hardware problem.

In 1969 the Data Processing Management Association named her the first computer science "Man of the Year," and she was awarded the National Medal of Technology in 1991.

to surveys conducted by the American Federation of Teachers, school districts report a considerable shortage of math teachers, with greater shortages occurring in large cities.

FOR MORE INFO

For more information on a teaching career, contact
American Federation of Teachers
555 New Jersey Avenue NW
Washington, DC 20001-2029
Tel: 202-879-4400
http://www.aft.org

For information on careers in mathematics, contact
American Mathematical Society
201 Charles Street
Providence, RI 02904-2213
Tel: 800-321-4AMS
http://www.ams.org

For information on teaching careers in mathematics, contact
National Council of Teachers of Mathematics
1906 Association Drive
Reston, VA 20191-1502
Tel: 703-620-9840
http://www.nctm.org

For information on public education, contact
National Education Association
1201 16th Street NW
Washington, DC 20036-3290
Tel: 202-833-4000
http://www.nea.org

Museum Attendants and Teachers

What Museum Attendants and Teachers Do

Museum attendants protect museum collections and help museum visitors. They are sometimes called *museum guards* because they protect the exhibits from harm. They inform visitors of museum rules and regulations. Sometimes this means preventing patrons from touching a display, or warning children not to run through the halls. If an exhibit is

Historical Facts

○ The term *museum* is from the ancient Greek word meaning "a place sacred to the Muses." The Muses were nine Roman goddesses who presided over literature, the arts, and the sciences.

○ The word museum was used for an institution for literary and scientific study founded in Alexandria, Egypt, in the third century B.C. The term came into use again in the fifteenth century. In Italy, scholars kept their collections of historical material in rooms they called museums. Renaissance nobles adorned their palaces with art, sculpture, and collections of curiosities. Later many private collections passed to public ownership and were put on display.

○ The British Museum, the first museum operated as a national institution, was founded in 1753.

○ The American Association of Museums was founded in 1906.

A museum teacher at the Virginia War Museum talks with visitors. The girl is wearing a nursing uniform worn by nurses in World War I. (Jeff Greenberg, The Image Works)

popular and draws a large crowd, museum attendants keep everyone orderly.

In some museums, the attendants may have to check the thermostats and climate controls. A priceless document or work of art can be destroyed as easily by humid conditions as by careless hands. Attendants report any damage or needed repairs to the *museum curator.*

Museum attendants are the main source of information for museum visitors. They know about the exhibits as well as the museum itself. Attendants answer questions from people of all ages and cultural backgrounds.

Most museums hold lectures, classes, workshops, and tours to teach the public about what is in

Did You Know?

○ There are approximately 17,500 museums in the United States.

○ Museums in the United States average approximately 865 million visits per year.

○ The most popular museum types in 2006 were: zoos, science and technology museums, arboretums and botanic gardens, children's and youth museums, and art museums.

Sources: American Association of Museums; Lake, Snell & Perry

the museum and why it is there. *Museum teachers* conduct all the educational programs. For special exhibits, the museum teacher works with the museum curator to develop written materials, such as pamphlets to be handed out at the display, books to be sold in the gift shop, or study guides for students. Museum teachers arrange and schedule classes for children and adults. They have strong communication skills and creativity to make these programs interesting to people of all ages and cultural backgrounds.

Education and Training

A high school diploma is required for museum attendants. Employers are more likely to hire those with college education or experience working in a museum. Attendants usually are trained on the job where they quickly learn about all the objects in the museum's permanent collection. They get additional training to learn about any special temporary exhibits.

Museum teachers need a college education with classes in education and a specialty. For example, teachers in art museums have studied art history and education. Many colleges offer courses in museum studies (museology), which are valuable in the competitive field of museum work.

Earnings

Large museums in big cities pay more than smaller regional museums. Salaries for museum attendants range from $9,000

EXPLORING

○ Read books about museums and career opportunities in the field.
○ Ask your guidance counselor to arrange an information interview with a museum attendant or teacher. Ask the following questions: What are your main and secondary job duties? What do you like least and most about your job? How did you train for this field? What advice would you give a young person who is interested in the field?
○ Participate in museum programs, such as field trips, photography clubs, study groups, and behind-the-scenes tours.
○ Talk to your local museum officials about any volunteer opportunities available.

FOR MORE INFO

For information on careers, education and training, and internships, contact

American Association of Museums
1575 Eye Street NW, Suite 400
Washington, DC 20005-1113
Tel: 202-289-1818
http://www.aam-us.org

This association for anyone interested in art education has student memberships.

National Art Education Association
1916 Association Drive
Reston, VA 20191-1590
Tel: 703-860-8000
E-mail: info@naea-reston.org
http://www.naea-reston.org

to $29,000 a year. Salaries for museum education specialists ranged from less than $31,595 to $57,233 or more in 2007, according to Salary.com.

Outlook

The education services provided by museum attendants and educators are an important part of a museum's operations. That means museums will expect greater professionalism, more education, and specialization in the future for high-level positions. Since budgets are small and often unstable, museums will depend on volunteer attendants and teachers. Competition for paid jobs will be stiff.

Music Teachers

What Music Teachers Do

Music teachers teach people how to sing, play musical instruments, and appreciate the world of music. They teach private lessons and classes. They may work at home or in a studio, school, college, or conservatory. Many music teachers are also performing musicians.

Teachers help students learn to read music, develop their voices, breathe correctly, and hold and play their instruments properly. As students master the techniques of their art, teachers guide them through more and more difficult pieces of music. Music teachers often organize recitals or concerts that feature their students.

Private music teachers may teach children who are just beginning to play or sing, teens who hope to make music their career, or adults who are interested in music lessons for their own enjoyment. They teach these students in a studio, in their homes, or at their students' homes.

Music teachers in elementary and secondary schools often offer group and private lessons. They direct in-school glee clubs, concert choirs, marching bands, or orchestras. College and university teachers are also frequently performers or composers. They divide their time between group and individual instruction and may teach several music subjects, such as music appreciation,

Popular Musical Instruments for Beginners

About.com lists the following instruments as the easiest to learn for beginners:

- ○ cello
- ○ clarinet
- ○ double bass
- ○ flute
- ○ guitar
- ○ harp
- ○ piano
- ○ saxophone
- ○ trumpet
- ○ violin

EXPLORING

○ Sing in your school or church choir. Join a band or orchestra. Get as much experience as you can playing, singing, and performing.

○ Read all you can about music theory, music history, famous musicians, and performance.

○ Talk to your music teachers about what they like and don't like about teaching music. Ask them how they became music teachers.

A music teacher gives a lesson to a student. (Dick Blume, Syracuse Newspapers, The Image Works)

music history, theory, and pedagogy (the teaching of music).

Education and Training

Participation in music classes, choral groups, bands, and orchestras is also good preparation for a music teaching career.

Like all musicians, music teachers spend years mastering their instruments or developing their voices. Private teachers need no formal training or licenses, but most have spent years studying with an experienced musician, either in a school or conservatory or through private lessons.

Teachers in elementary schools and high schools must have a state-issued teaching license. There are about 600 conservatories, universities, and colleges that offer bachelor's degrees in music education to qualify students for state certificates.

To teach music in colleges and schools of music or in conservatories, you must usually have a graduate degree in music. However, very talented and well-known performers or composers are sometimes hired without any formal graduate training.

Earnings

Salaries for music teachers vary depending on the type of teaching, the number of hours spent teaching, and the skill

Methods for Teaching Music

There are several well-known methods for teaching music to young children.

1. The Suzuki method was begun in the mid-1900s by Japanese violinist Shinichi Suzuki (1898–1998). He believed that the best way to learn music is to be exposed to it from a very early age. He thought young children should learn to play an instrument in the same way that they learn to speak and read—by listening, absorbing, and copying.

In the beginning, the parent is given the first lessons on the instrument, while the child watches. In this way, the child becomes interested in copying the parent. When the child begins learning, it is by ear. Music reading is taught later, at about the same age a child learns to read books.

2. The Orff-Schulwerk system for teaching music to children was started by Carl Orff (1895–1982). Orff believed that music was connected with movement, dance, and speech.

Orff-Schulwerk uses poems, rhymes, games, songs, and dances as examples and basic materials. Improvisation and composition are key to learning and appreciating music.

3. The Kodaly philosophy is based on the work of Zoltan Kodaly (1882–1967). He believed it was important for children to sing, play instruments, and dance from memory. Children start learning traditional songs, games, chants, and folk songs and later learn the music of other cultures and countries.

The Kodaly method also involves performing, listening to, and analyzing the great art music of the world, as well as mastering musical skills.

---

of the teacher. According to the National Association for Music Education, early childhood music educators earn $6 to $60 per hour, while studio music teachers earn $10 to $100 per hour. Full-time music teachers at the elementary and secondary levels earn salaries that range from $19,000 to $70,000 annually. The U.S. Department of Labor reports that college music, art, and drama teachers earned median annual salaries of $53,160 in 2006.

Outlook

Opportunities for music teachers are expected to grow at an average rate in elementary schools and colleges and universities, but at a slower rate in secondary schools. When schools face budgetary problems, music and other art programs are often the first to be cut.

FOR MORE INFO

To read about the issues affecting teachers, contact the following organizations:

American Federation of Teachers
555 New Jersey Avenue NW
Washington, DC 20001-2029
Tel: 202-879-4400
http://www.aft.org

National Education Association
1201 16th Street NW
Washington, DC 20036-3290
Tel: 202-833-4000
http://www.nea.org

For information on string and orchestra teaching and playing, contact

American String Teachers Association
4153 Chain Bridge Road
Fairfax, VA 22030-4102
Tel: 703-279-2113
E-mail: asta@astaweb.com
http://www.astaweb.com

For information on music education, contact

Music Teachers National Association
441 Vine Street, Suite 3100
Cincinnati, OH 45202-3004
Tel: 888-512-5278
http://www.mtna.org

Naturalists

What Naturalists Do

Naturalists study the natural world in order to learn the best way to preserve the Earth and its living creatures—humans, animals, and plants. They teach the public about the environment and show people what they can do about such hazards as pollution.

Naturalists may work in wildlife museums, private nature centers, or large zoos. Some naturalists work for parks, most of which are operated by state or federal governments. Naturalists also can work as *nature resource managers, wildlife conservationists, ecologists,* and *environmental educators* for many different employers.

Depending on where they work, naturalists may protect and conserve wildlife or particular kinds of land, such as prairie or

The Beginnings of Conservation

During the nineteenth century in the United States, many great forests were cut down and huge areas of land were leveled for open-pit mining and quarrying. More disease occurred with the increase of air pollution from the smokestacks of factories, home chimneys, and engine exhaust. At the same time there was a dramatic decrease in populations of elk, antelope, deer, bison, and other animals of the Great Plains. Some types of bear, cougar, and wolf became extinct, as well as several kinds of birds, such as the passenger pigeon. In the latter half of the nineteenth century, the government set up a commission to develop scientific management of fisheries. It established the first national park (Yellowstone National Park in Wyoming, Idaho, and Montana), and set aside the first forest reserves. These early steps led to the modern conservation movement.

EXPLORING

○ Read books and magazines about nature and work of naturalists. One interesting publication is *The American Naturalist,* published by the University of Chicago Press for the American Society of Naturalists. Visit http://www.journals.uchicago.edu/AN/home.html to read sample articles.

○ Visit your local nature centers and park preserves often. Attend any classes or special lectures they offer. There may be opportunities to volunteer to help clean up sites, plant trees, or maintain pathways and trails.

○ Hiking, birdwatching, and photography are good hobbies for future naturalists.

○ Get to know your local wildlife. What kind of insects, birds, fish, and other animals live in your area? Your librarian will be able to help you find books that identify local flora and fauna.

wetlands. Other naturalists research and carry out plans to restore lands that have been damaged by erosion, fire, or development. Some naturalists re-create wildlife habitats and nature trails. They plant trees, for example, or label existing plants. *Fish and wildlife wardens* help regulate populations of fish, hunted animals, and protected animals. They control hunting and fishing and make sure species are thriving but not overpopulating their territories. *Wildlife managers, range managers,* and *conservationists* also maintain the plant and animal life in a certain area. They work in parks or on ranges that have both domestic livestock and wild animals. They test soil and water for nutrients and pollution. They count plant and animal populations each season.

Naturalists do some indoor work. They raise funds for projects, write reports, keep detailed records, and write articles, brochures, and newsletters to educate the public about their work. They might campaign for support for protection of an endangered species by holding meetings and hearings. Other public education activities include giving tours, leading nature walks, and offering demonstrations and classes.

Education and Training

If you are interested in this field, you should take a number of basic science courses in high school, including biology,

A naturalist shows plants to children at a summer camp. (Jeff Greenberg, The Image Works)

chemistry, and earth science. Botany courses and clubs are also helpful, since they provide direct experience monitoring plant growth and health.

Some Pioneer Naturalists

Ralph Waldo Emerson (1803–1882) was an American philosopher and author. He helped form and promote the philosophy known as Transcendentalism, which emphasizes the spiritual dimension in nature and in all persons.

Henry David Thoreau (1817–1862) was an American author. His *Walden* (1854) is a classic of American literature. It tells about the two years he lived in a small cabin on the shore of Walden Pond near Concord, Massachusetts. In *Walden*, he described the changing seasons and other natural events and scenes that he observed.

Gilbert White (1720–1793) was an English minister. While living and working in his native village of Selborne (southwest of London), White became a careful observer of its natural setting. He corresponded with important British naturalists and eventually published *The Natural History and Antiquities of Selborne*.

Naturalists must have at least a bachelor's degree in biology, zoology, chemistry, botany, natural history, or environmental science. A master's degree is not a requirement, but is useful. Many naturalists have a master's degree in education. Experience gained through summer jobs and volunteer work can be just as important as educational requirements. Background working with the public is also helpful.

Earnings

Starting salaries for full-time naturalists range from about $20,000 to $29,000 per year. Some part-time workers, however, make as little as minimum wage. For some positions, housing and vehicles may

FOR MORE INFO

For information on careers, contact
American Society of Naturalists
http://www.amnat.org

U.S. Bureau of Land Management
U.S. Department of the Interior
1849 C Street, Room 406-LS
Washington, DC 20240-0002
Tel: 202-452-5125
http://www.blm.gov

For information on conservation and environmental education, contact
National Wildlife Federation
11100 Wildlife Center Drive
Reston, VA 20190-5361
Tel: 800-822-9919
http://www.nwf.org

North American Association for Environmental Education
2000 P Street NW, Suite 540
Washington, DC 20036-6921
Tel: 202-419-0412
http://www.naaee.org

Student Conservation Association
PO Box 550
Charlestown, NC 03603-0550
Tel: 603-543-1700
http://www.sca-inc.org

For information on careers, contact
U.S. Fish and Wildlife Service
U.S. Department of the Interior
Division of Human Resources
4401 North Fairfax Drive, MS-2000
Arlington, VA 22203-1610
http://hr.fws.gov/HR/Careers_FWS.htm

be provided. Earnings vary for those with added responsibilities or advanced degrees. The U.S. Department of Labor reports that conservation scientists (a category that includes naturalists) earned a median annual salary of $54,970 in 2006. Salaries ranged from less than $29,860 to $80,260 or more.

Outlook

In the next decade, the job outlook for naturalists is expected to be only fair, despite the public's increasing environmental awareness. Private nature centers and preserves—where forests, wetlands, and prairies are restored—are continuing to open in the United States, but possible government cutbacks in nature programs may limit their growth. Competition will be quite high, since there are many qualified people entering this field.

Preschool Teachers

What Preschool Teachers Do

Preschool teachers teach children who are between two and four years old. They work in child care centers, nursery schools, Head Start programs, and other private and public programs. They prepare children for kindergarten and grade school by teaching them the letters, numbers, colors, and days of the week, and by introducing them to telling time. Preschool teachers also introduce children to books, educational games, and computer software. They also teach students social skills through play and activities.

In preschool classrooms, teachers plan and lead activities like storytelling, arts and crafts projects, and singing, depending on the abilities and interests of the children. For example, to teach children about using the senses, telling time, or writing the alphabet, they might use finger painting, puppets, music, or games. Teachers have to think about which skills children

Young Children Learn Through Work

Young children can do many chores around the house that teach them to be responsible and independent. Christine A. Readdick and Kathy Douglas, authors of "More Than Line Leader and Door Holder: Engaging Young Children in Real Work," an article in the journal *Young Children,* report that children are eager to help adults and that this work is an important part of early learning.

Some people object to making children work, but Readdick and Douglas suggest that children can learn a lot from helping to gather, prepare, and cook food; running errands; doing light housekeeping chores; caring for pets; or gardening.

A preschool teacher reads a book to children during story time. (Ellen B. Senisi, The Image Works)

should be learning at a particular age. They encourage the children to think creatively and to express their feelings and ideas. They help them develop social skills as they adjust to being in school with other children, and introduce them to the concepts of sharing and playing in groups. Other social skills might include manners, hygiene, and cleaning up after themselves.

Preschool teachers also get to know the children's parents and regularly provide them with reports on progress and behavior. They might also invite parents along on field trips, and to the classroom to observe.

Education and Training

In high school, you should take child development, home economics, and

EXPLORING

- There are many volunteer opportunities for working with kids. Check with your library or local literacy program about tutoring children and reading to preschoolers.
- Summer day camps or church schools with preschool classes may offer assistant or aide opportunities.
- Babysitting is a good way to get child care experience.
- Teach a younger sister or brother letters, numbers, and colors. Help your sibling learn to read or tell time.

To Be a Successful Preschool Teacher, You Should . . .

○ be a good role model

○ be respectful of children

○ have a good sense of humor

○ be patient

○ be a good communicator

○ have good organizational skills

other classes that involve you with child care, such as family and consumer science classes. You'll also need an understanding of the general subjects you'll be introducing to preschool students, so take English, science, and math. Also, take classes in art, music, and theater to develop your creative skills.

Large child care centers sometimes hire high school graduates with some child care experience and provide on-the-job training. For example, the American Montessori Society offers a career program for aspiring preschool teachers.

Some schools require preschool teachers to have bachelor's degrees. There are many colleges and universities that offer programs in early childhood education and child care.

Earnings

Salaries in this profession tend to be lower than for teaching positions in public elementary and high schools. Because some preschool programs are held only in the morning or afternoon, many preschool teachers work only part time. As part-time workers, preschool teachers may earn as little as minimum wage to start.

According to the U.S. Department of Labor, preschool teachers earned a median salary of $22,680 a year in 2006. Annual salaries for these workers ranged from less than $14,870 to $39,960 or more.

Outlook

Employment opportunities for preschool teachers are expected to increase faster than the average, according to the U.S. Department of Labor. Specific job opportunities vary from state to state. Jobs should be available at private child care centers, nursery schools, Head Start facilities, and laboratory schools connected with universities and colleges. In the past, the majority of preschool teachers were female, and although this continues to be the case, more males are becoming involved in early childhood education.

FOR MORE INFO

For information on training programs, contact
American Montessori Society
281 Park Avenue South, 6th Floor
New York, NY 10010-6125
Tel: 212-358-1250
E-mail: info@amshq.org
http://www.amshq.org

For information on certification, contact
Council for Professional Recognition
2460 16th Street NW
Washington, DC 20009-3575
Tel: 800-424-4310
http://www.cdacouncil.org

For more information about preschool teachers and accredited training programs, contact
National Association for the Education of Young Children
1313 L Street NW, Suite 500
Washington, DC 20005-4110
Tel: 800-424-2460
http://www.naeyc.org

For information about student memberships and training opportunities, contact
National Association of Child Care Professionals
PO Box 90723
Austin, TX 78709-0723
Tel: 800-537-1118
E-mail: admin@naccp.org
http://www.naccp.org

School Administrators

What School Administrators Do

School administrators oversee the operation of schools or entire school districts. They work with either public or private schools. Those working as administrators in private schools are often called *headmasters* (or *headmistresses)* or *school directors.* They make sure students, teachers, and other employees follow educational guidelines as well as monitor the school's budget.

There are two basic kinds of school administrators in public schools: *principals* and *superintendents.* School principals supervise teachers and make sure they are using approved teaching methods. They visit classrooms and examine learning materials. They also supervise the school's counselors and other staff members. They review the students' performance and decide how to handle students with learning or behavioral problems. In larger schools, there may also be an *assistant principal,* sometimes called the *dean of students.*

School superintendents are responsible for an entire school district. They are appointed by the board of education to see that the district's schools meet their standards. Superintendents have many duties. They hire staff, settle labor disputes,

Women in School Administration

According to studies by the American Association of School Administrators, more than 20 percent of school superintendents are women—up from 6.6 percent in 1992. The study also showed that more than half of the students in education administration programs are women.

formulate the district's budget, oversee school bus service, speak to community groups, purchase school supplies, and ensure that school buildings are maintained and repaired.

Education and Training

In high school, take a wide range of college preparatory courses, including English, mathematics, science, music, art, and history. Computer science and business classes will also be beneficial.

Most principals and assistant principals have had years of teaching experience and hold master's degrees in educational administration. Guidance counselors, resource center directors, and other staff members also may be promoted to the position of principal.

A doctorate in educational administration is often required for school superintendents. Large school districts may also want their superintendents to have a law or business degree. All school superintendents need to have previous experience as administrators in some field.

EXPLORING

Before you can become a principal or superintendent, you need teaching experience. You can gain experience in education by:

○ teaching religious school classes
○ working as a summer camp counselor or day care center aide
○ working with a scouting group
○ volunteering to coach a youth athletic team
○ tutoring younger students

To Be a Successful School Administrator, You Should . . .

○ have strong leadership skills
○ have good communication skills
○ be able to get along with people of many different ages and types
○ be self-motivated
○ have confidence
○ be able to accept constructive criticism

FOR MORE INFO

For information on the career of school administrator, contact
American Association of School Administrators
801 North Quincy Street, Suite 700
Arlington, VA 22203-1730
Tel: 703-528-0700
E-mail: info@aasa.org
http://www.aasa.org

For information on careers at the elementary level, contact
National Association of Elementary School Principals
1615 Duke Street
Alexandria, VA 22314-3406
Tel: 800-386-2377
E-mail: naesp@naesp.org
http://www.naesp.org

For information on careers at the secondary level, contact
National Association of Secondary School Principals
1904 Association Drive
Reston, VA 20191-1537
Tel: 703-860-0200
http://www.nassp.org

Earnings

The U.S. Department of Labor reports that the median annual earnings of education administrators were $73,990 in 2006. Salaries ranged from less than $41,120 to $137,900 or more. School administrators employed by elementary and secondary schools earned median salaries of $77,740.

Outlook

Employment for school administrators is expected to grow about as fast as the average, according to the U.S. Department of Labor. Opportunities will be good because a large number of administrators are expected to retire or change jobs. There is a shortage of qualified candidates to fill those positions. More than half of working superintendents don't have doctoral degrees, but many school boards prefer candidates with doctorates, so the standards will be higher for applicants. There is also a shortage of people with the desired qualifications who are interested in these positions. Many qualified people view school administration as too political, consider the pay low, and feel discouraged by the restrictions on moving between districts.

The American Association of School Administrators reports that a new career is developing to handle the shortage. A number of districts have hired interim superintendents as temporary replacements until they can find a permanent candidate.

Secondary School Teachers

What Secondary School Teachers Do

Secondary school teachers instruct junior and senior high school students. They usually specialize in a certain subject, such as English, mathematics, biology, or history. In addition to classroom instruction, they plan lessons, prepare tests, grade papers, complete report cards, meet with parents, and supervise other activities. They often meet individually with students to discuss homework assignments, or academic or personal problems.

Depending on the subject, teachers may use a variety of teaching techniques, including lectures, films, photographs, readings, guest speakers, discussions, and demonstrations. They interact

The First Secondary Schools

Early secondary education was typically based upon training students to enter the clergy. Benjamin Franklin pioneered the idea of the academy, a broader secondary education that offered a flexible curriculum and a wide variety of academic subjects.

It was not until the nineteenth century that children of different social classes commonly attended school into the secondary grades. The first English Classical School was established in 1821 in Boston.

The junior high school was the idea of Dr. Charles W. Eliot, president of Harvard. In 1888, he recommended that secondary studies be started two years earlier than was the custom. The first junior high school opened in 1908, in Columbus, Ohio.

By the early twentieth century, secondary school attendance was made mandatory in the United States.

EXPLORING

○ If you are in high school, you've already gained a good sense of the daily work of a secondary school teacher. But the requirements of a teacher go far beyond the classroom, so ask to spend some time with one of your teachers after school, and ask to look at lecture notes and record-keeping procedures.

○ Volunteer for a peer tutoring program. Other opportunities that will give you teaching experience include coaching an athletic team at the YMCA or YWCA, counseling at a summer camp, teaching an art course at a community center, or assisting with a community theater production.

with the students and ask and answer questions to make sure everyone understands the lessons. In order to reinforce the material taught in class, they assign homework, give tests, and assign projects that help students develop an understanding of the content.

Some secondary school teachers are specially trained to work with students who have disabilities. Others teach advanced lessons for students with high grades and achievement scores.

Secondary school teachers have many responsibilities outside of the classroom, as well. They keep grade and attendance records. They prepare lesson plans, exams, and homework assignments. In between classes, they oversee study halls and supervise lunchroom activities. They attend school meetings or meet with parents and students. They may supervise extracurricular activities like sports teams, the school newspaper, or the drama club.

Education and Training

Secondary school teachers must have at least a bachelor's degree as well as a credential from an approved teacher-training program. Many colleges and universities offer these programs in their education departments. You must take courses in the subject area you want to teach, as well as a number of education courses covering teaching techniques and related subjects. You must also spend several months as a student teacher under the supervision of an experienced teacher. Upon completion of the program, you receive certification as a secondary school teacher. Many teachers go on to earn master's degrees in education or in the subject that they wish to teach.

All teachers must be certified before beginning work in a public school, and many school systems require additional qualifications. While working, teachers must often attend education conferences and summer workshops to maintain certification and further their training.

Earnings

According to the U.S. Department of Labor, the median annual salary for secondary school teachers was $47,740 in 2006. The lowest 10 percent earned less than $31,760; the highest 10 percent earned $76,100 or more. According to the American Federation of Teachers, beginning teachers earned average salaries of $31,753 in 2004–2005.

Outlook

The U.S. Department of Labor predicts that employment for secondary teachers will grow about as fast as the average. New teachers will be needed to meet rising enrollments and to replace the large number of teachers who are retiring or

Salary Timeline

The American Federation of Teachers' first salary survey in 1948–1949 polled 1.25 million teachers. Salaries averaged under $3,000 a year.

During the 1960s, wages for teachers increased. In 1964–1965, the national average salary for a teacher was $6,195. By 1972–1973, the national average teacher salary increased to $10,176.

The average salary for today's 3 million teachers is $47,602, tens of thousands of dollars less per year than their peers earn in other professions. These low salaries are having a serious impact on the ability of school districts around the country to attract the best candidates into the teaching profession.

leaving the field. The National Education Association believes this will be a challenge because of the low salaries that secondary school teachers earn. In addition to higher salaries, smaller class sizes and safer schools will be necessary to attract new teachers and retain experienced ones.

FOR MORE INFO

To read about the issues affecting teachers, contact the following organizations:

American Federation of Teachers
555 New Jersey Avenue NW
Washington, DC 20001-2029
Tel: 202-879-4400
http://www.aft.org

National Education Association
1201 16th Street NW
Washington, DC 20036-3290
Tel: 202-833-4000
http://www.nea.org

Special Education Teachers

What Special Education Teachers Do

Special education teachers work with students who need special attention, including those who have physical, developmental, behavioral, or learning disabilities, as well as those who are gifted and talented. They create individual programs for each student. They work closely with students to determine their learning and skill levels, and they work with school psychologists, social workers, occupational and physical therapists, and speech-language therapists.

Some students have learning disabilities that prevent them from learning through usual teaching methods. They may need instruction at a slower pace or in quiet, nondistracting settings. Teachers may need to read assignments aloud to them and to help them focus their attention on schoolwork.

Some students have emotional or behavioral problems. Others are considered below average in their mental abilities. Some students are language impaired, which means they have

Special Ed Letters

ADA Americans with Disabilities Act

ADD Attention Deficit Disorder

ADHD Attention Deficit Hyperactivity Disorder

ASL American Sign Language

B/VI blind/visually impaired

CLD culturally or linguistically different

DD developmentally delayed

D/HI deaf/hearing impaired

ED emotionally disturbed

IDEA Individuals with Disabilities Educational Act

IEP individualized education plan

LD learning disabled

MG mentally gifted

MR mental retardation

NI neurologically impaired

OHI other health impaired

PH physically handicapped

A special education teacher reads a book to a boy with Down's syndrome. (Bob Daemmrich, The Image Works)

EXPLORING

○ To learn more about disabilities, visit http://soeweb.syr.edu/thechp/disres.htm, which has links to a variety of resources.

○ Become involved in a school or community mentoring program for students with special needs. There may also be other opportunities for volunteer work or part-time jobs with community agencies, camps, and residential facilities.

○ Get to know special-needs students at your school.

○ Learn to use sign language or read braille.

trouble communicating. Special education teachers work with students who are visually impaired or blind, and hard of hearing or deaf. They also help students with physical handicaps such as muscle, nerve, or bone disorders. When working with physically handicapped students, teachers may use special equipment, such as computers that are operated by touching a screen or by voice commands, or books in braille.

Most special education teachers work in public schools. Some, however, work in local education agencies, colleges and universities, and private schools. They may spend their days in specially equipped classrooms, ordinary classrooms, therapy rooms, and clinics.

Education and Training

College preparatory courses in English, science, math, and government will help you prepare for this career. Speech and sign language courses will develop good communication skills and psychology courses will help you understand some of the learning problems your students face.

The requirements for becoming a special education teacher are similar to those for becoming an elementary or secondary school teacher, but may involve a longer period of training. All states require teachers to earn a bachelor's degree that includes specific education courses.

Many states require an additional year or two of graduate study and some states require a master's degree in special education. You also must be certified by your state, which may involve passing an exam. In addition, you must complete one or more semesters of student teaching in order to gain first-hand experience in a classroom under the guidance of a certified teacher.

Learn More About It

Corwin, Miles. *And Still We Rise: The Trials and Triumphs of Twelve Gifted Inner-City Students.* New York: Harper Perennial, 2001.

Sabin, Ellen. *The Autism Acceptance Book: Being a Friend to Someone with Autism.* New York: Watering Can Press, 2006.

————. *The Special Needs Acceptance Book: Being a Friend to Someone with Special Needs.* New York: Watering Can Press, 2007.

Sinisi, Ellen B. *Visiting a Class for Children with Special Needs.* New York: Dutton Juvenile, 1998.

Stern, Judith, and Uzi Ben-Ami. *Many Ways to Learn: Young People's Guide to Learning Disabilities.* Washington, D.C.: Magination Press, 1996.

FOR MORE INFO

For information on current issues in special education, contact

Council of Administrators of Special Education
Fort Valley State University
1005 State University Drive
Fort Valley, GA 31030-4313
Tel: 478-825-7667
http://www.casecec.org

For information on careers, contact

National Association of Special Education Teachers
1250 Connecticut Avenue NW, Suite 200
Washington DC 20036-2643
Tel: 800-754-4421
E-mail: contactus@naset.org
http://www.naset.org

For information on careers in special education, contact

National Clearinghouse for Professions in Special Education
http://www.special-ed-careers.org

For information on special education programs sponsored by the federal government, contact

U.S. Department of Education
Office of Special Education and Rehabilitative Services
400 Maryland Avenue SW
Washington, DC 20202-7100
Tel: 202-245-7468
http://www.ed.gov/about/offices/list/osers/index.html

Earnings

According to the U.S. Department of Labor, salaries for special education teachers ranged from less than $31,320 to more than $80,170 in 2006. Preschools and elementary schools paid an average of $46,360; middle schools, $47,650; and secondary schools, $48,330. Private school teachers usually earn lower salaries than public school teachers.

Outlook

The field of special education is expected to grow faster than the average, according to the U.S. Department of Labor. This demand is caused partly by the growth in the number of special education students needing services. Because of the rise in the number of youths with disabilities under the age of 21, the government has approved more federally funded programs. Growth of jobs in this field has also been influenced positively by legislation in favor of training and employment for individuals with disabilities and a growing public awareness and interest in those with disabilities.

Teacher Aides

What Teacher Aides Do

Teachers plan and teach lessons, grade papers, prepare exams, attend faculty meetings, and perform a variety of other duties. *Teacher aides* assist them in many of their responsibilities. Teacher aides are sometimes called *education paraprofessionals* or *paraeducators.*

Teacher aides help prepare instructional materials for students, assist students with their classroom work, and supervise lunchrooms, playgrounds, hallways, and other areas around the school. They also do paperwork, grade students' tests, and operate audiovisual equipment. They take attendance and distribute materials such as books, photocopies, and writing supplies.

Teacher aides make sure students get on the correct school bus after school ends, and they stay with other students until parents and carpool drivers arrive. They help teachers with filing, word processing, and photocopying. Aides write requests for classroom supplies and help arrange class trips.

Teacher aides do some teaching. They give lectures, conduct group discussions, and listen to elementary school children read. They help run school projects, such

Names and Places

Today, more than 1.3 education paraprofessionals work under job titles such as:

- teacher aide or assistant
- instructional aide or assistant
- special education assistant
- preschool or early childhood assistant
- bilingual assistant
- library assistant

Education paraprofessionals work in a variety of settings that include:

- preschools and day care centers
- elementary schools
- junior and senior high schools
- vocational education centers
- community colleges
- adult education programs

EXPLORING

○ Read books and magazines about teaching.

○ Volunteer to help with religious education classes at your place of worship.

○ Volunteer to help with scouting troops or work as a counselor at a summer day camp.

○ Volunteer to help coach a children's athletic team or work with children in after-school programs at community centers.

○ Babysitting will give you experience in working with children and help you learn about the different stages of child development.

○ Talk to teacher aides in your school about their careers.

as science fairs or theater productions, and assist teachers on field trips to museums and zoos.

Teacher aides work in traditional schools and classrooms, in special education, bilingual education, and a variety of other settings. They most often work in elementary schools, but teacher aides also work in high schools, often with students who have learning disabilities or behavioral disorders. They often work in classes that have a large number of students or one or more students with disabilities.

Education and Training

To be a teacher aide, you need a well-rounded education in math, English, science, art, and physical education. Courses in child development, home economics, and sociology are valuable in this career. Educational requirements for teacher aides vary widely.

To Be a Successful Teacher Aide, You Should . . .

○ enjoy working with children

○ be able to follow instructions, but also work on your own, when needed

○ have a flexible, cheerful personality

○ have strong communication skills

A teacher aide helps a student during a math lesson. (David Bacon, The Image Works)

Teacher aides who handle clerical or supervisory duties only need a high school diploma. If you will be doing any teaching or classroom work, however, some college work is usually required.

Teacher aides often receive on-the-job training, often under the supervision of a certified teacher.

Earnings

Teacher aides are usually paid on an hourly basis and usually only during the nine or 10 months of the school calendar. Salaries vary depending upon the school or district, the region of the country, and the duties performed. Median annual earnings of teacher assistants were $20,740 in 2006, according to the U.S. Department of Labor. Salaries ranged from less than $13,910 to more than $31,610.

Outlook

Employment in this field is expected to grow about as fast as the average because of an expected increase in the number of

FOR MORE INFO

To learn about current issues affecting para-professionals in education, contact
American Federation of Teachers
555 New Jersey Avenue NW
Washington, DC 20001-2029
Tel: 202-879-4400
http://www.aft.org

To order publications and to read current research and other information, contact
Association for Childhood Education International
17904 Georgia Avenue, Suite 215
Olney, MD 20832-2277
Tel: 800-423-3563
E-mail: headquarters@acei.org
http://www.acei.org

For information about training programs and other resources, contact
National Resource Center for Paraprofessionals
http://www.nrcpara.org

students with special needs and students for whom English is not their first language.

As the number of students in schools increases, new schools and classrooms will be added and more teachers and teacher aides will be hired. An expected shortage of teachers means that administrators will hire more aides to help with larger classrooms.

Because of increased responsibilities for aides, state departments of education will likely establish standards of training in the near future. The National Resource Center for Paraprofessionals has created national standards for para-educator training.

Glossary

accredited approved as meeting established standards for providing good training and education; this approval is usually given by an independent organization of professionals

apprentice a person who is learning a trade by working under the supervision of a skilled worker; apprentices often receive classroom instruction in addition to their supervised practical experience

associate's degree an academic rank or title granted by a community or junior college or similar institution to graduates of a two-year program of education beyond high school

bachelor's degree an academic rank or title given to a person who has completed a four-year program of study at a college or university; also called an undergraduate degree or baccalaureate

career an occupation for which a worker receives training and has an opportunity for advancement

certified approved as meeting established requirements for skill, knowledge, and experience in a particular field; people are certified by the organization of professionals in their field

college a higher education institution that is above the high school level

community college a public or private two-year college attended by students who do not usually live at the college; graduates of a community college receive an associate's degree and may transfer to a four-year college or university to complete a bachelor's degree

diploma   a certificate or document given by a school to show that a person has completed a course or has graduated from the school

distance education   a type of educational program that allows students to take classes and complete their education by mail or the Internet

doctorate   the highest academic rank or title granted by a graduate school to a person who has completed a two- to three-year program after having received a master's degree

fringe benefit   a payment or benefit to an employee in addition to regular wages or salary; examples of fringe benefits include a pension, a paid vacation, and health or life insurance

graduate school   a school that people may attend after they have received their bachelor's degree; people who complete an educational program at a graduate school earn a master's degree or a doctorate

intern   an advanced student (usually one with at least some college training) in a professional field who is employed in a job that is intended to provide supervised practical experience for the student

internship   (1) the position or job of an intern; (2) the period of time when a person is an intern

junior college   a two-year college that offers courses like those in the first half of a four-year college program; graduates of a junior college usually receive an associate's degree and may transfer to a four-year college or university to complete a bachelor's degree

liberal arts   the subjects covered by college courses that develop broad general knowledge rather than specific occupational skills; the liberal arts often include philosophy, literature and the arts, history, language, and some courses in the social sciences and natural sciences

licensed   having formal permission from the proper authority to carry out an activity that would be illegal without that permission;

for example, a person must be licensed to practice medicine or drive a car

major the academic field in which a college student specializes and receives a degree

master's degree an academic rank or title granted by a graduate school to a person who has completed a one- or two-year program after having received a bachelor's degree

pension an amount of money paid regularly by an employer to a former employee after he or she retires from working

scholarship a gift of money to a student to help the student pay for further education

social studies courses of study (such as civics, geography, and history) that deal with how human societies work

starting salary salary paid to a newly hired employee; the starting salary is usually a smaller amount than is paid to a more experienced worker

technical college a private or public college offering two- or four-year programs in technical subjects; technical colleges offer courses in both general and technical subjects and award associate's degrees and bachelor's degrees

technician a worker with specialized practical training in a mechanical or scientific subject who works under the supervision of scientists, engineers, or other professionals; technicians typically receive two years of college-level education after high school

technologist a worker in a mechanical or scientific field with more training than a technician; technologists typically must have between two and four years of college-level education after high school

undergraduate a student at a college or university who has not yet received a degree

undergraduate degree   see **bachelor's degree**

union   an organization whose members are workers in a particular industry or company; the union works to gain better wages, benefits, and working conditions for its members; also called a labor union or trade union

vocational school   a public or private school that offers training in one or more skills or trades

wage   money that is paid in return for work done, especially money paid on the basis of the number of hours or days worked

Index of Job Titles

Browse and Learn More

Books

Edelfelt, Roy, and Alan Reiman. *Careers in Education.* 4th ed. New York: McGraw-Hill, 2003.

Fine, Janet. *Opportunities in Teaching Careers.* New York: McGraw-Hill, 2005.

Gisler, Margaret M. *101 Career Alternatives for Teachers: Exciting Job Opportunities for Teachers Outside the Teaching Profession.* New York: Three Rivers, 2002.

Horowitz, Jennifer A. *What Can You Do with a Major in Education?* Hoboken, N.J.: Cliffs Notes, 2005.

Peterson's. *Peterson's Summer Opportunities for Kids & Teenagers.* 24th ed. Lawrenceville, N.J.: Peterson's, 2006.

Rowh, Mark. *Opportunities in Educational Support Careers.* New York: McGraw-Hill, 2001.

Web Sites

American Association of Colleges for Teacher Education
http://www.aacte.org

American Association of Community Colleges
http://www.aacc.nche.edu

American Association of University Professors
http://www.aaup.org/aaup

American Federation of Teachers: Becoming a Teacher
http://www.aft.org/teachers/jft/becoming.htm

American Library Association: Great Web Sites for Kids
http://www.ala.org/greatsites

Distance Education and Training Council
http://www.detc.org

National Association for the Education of Young Children
http://www.naeyc.org

National Council for Accreditation of Teacher Education: Current and Future Teachers
http://www.ncate.org/public/CurrentFutureTeacher.asp

National Education Association
http://www.nea.org

Teach For America
http://www.teachforamerica.org

U.S. Department of Education
http://www.ed.gov/index.jhtml